T0331042

Financial Derivatives

Futures, Forwards, Swaps, Options, Corporate Securities, and Credit Default Swaps

World Scientific Lecture Notes in Economics

ISSN: 2382-6118

Series Editor: Dirk Bergemann *(Yale University, USA)*

Vol. 1: Financial Derivatives: Futures, Forwards, Swaps, Options, Corporate
        Securities, and Credit Default Swaps
        by George M. Constantinides

Forthcoming:

Lecture Notes on Econometric Models for Industrial Organization
   by Matthew Shum

Cooperature Game Theory
   by Adam Brandenburger

Economics of the Middle East
   by Julia C. Devlin

World Scientific Lecture Notes in Economics – Vol. 1

Financial Derivatives

Futures, Forwards, Swaps, Options, Corporate
Securities, and Credit Default Swaps

George M Constantinides

University of Chicago Booth School of Business, USA

World Scientific

NEW JERSEY · LONDON · SINGAPORE · BEIJING · SHANGHAI · HONG KONG · TAIPEI · CHENNAI

Published by

World Scientific Publishing Co. Pte. Ltd.
5 Toh Tuck Link, Singapore 596224
USA office: 27 Warren Street, Suite 401-402, Hackensack, NJ 07601
UK office: 57 Shelton Street, Covent Garden, London WC2H 9HE

Library of Congress Cataloging-in-Publication Data
Constantinides, George M.
    Financial derivatives : futures, forwards, swaps, options, corporate securities and credit default swaps / by George M Constantinides (University of Chicago Booth School of Business, USA).
    pages cm. -- (World scientific lecture notes in economics, ISSN 2382-6118 ; vol. 1)
    Includes bibliographical references and index.
    ISBN 978-9814618410 (hardcover : alk. paper)
    ISBN 9789814618427 (pbk. : alk. paper)
    1. Derivative securities. 2. Options (Finance) 3. Swaps (Finance) I. Title.
    HG6024.A3C663 2015
    332.64'57--dc23
                                                    2014041576

British Library Cataloguing-in-Publication Data
A catalogue record for this book is available from the British Library.

In-house Editors: Parvath Radha/Philly Lim

Typeset by Stallion Press
Email: enquiries@stallionpress.com

Printed in Singapore

To my students and colleagues from whom I learned a great deal
and who helped me build these teaching notes.

Contents

About the Author

 The Leo Melamed Professor of Finance at the University of Chicago's Booth School of Business, George Constantinides is a leader of academic finance, an expert in portfolio theory, asset pricing, derivatives pricing, and capital markets behavior. Widely published and a frequent speaker and editor, he is former president of the American Finance Association and the Society for Financial Studies and member of Dimensional's Boards of Directors of the US mutual funds, among many other professional affiliations. A graduate of Oxford University in England and Indiana University, he has also visited at Harvard University.

Preface

Derivatives markets are an important and growing segment of financial markets and play an important role in the management of risk. This invaluable set of lecture notes is meant to be used in conjunction with a standard textbook on derivatives in an advanced undergraduate or MBA elective course on futures, forwards, swaps, options, corporate securities, and credit default swaps (CDS). It covers the foundations of derivatives pricing in arbitrage-free markets, develops the methodology of risk-neutral valuation, and discusses hedging and the management of risk.

I develop, critically assess, and apply theories of pricing derivatives. Topics include: Introduction to forward contracts, futures, and swaps; pricing forwards and futures; interest rate and currency swaps; introduction to options and no-arbitrage restrictions; trading strategies and slope and convexity restrictions; optimal early exercise of American options; binomial option pricing; risk-neutral valuation; the Black–Scholes–Merton option pricing formula; extensions of the BSM model; risk management with options; empirical evidence and time-varying volatility; the pricing and hedging of corporate securities (common stock, senior and junior bonds, callable bonds, warrants, convertible bonds, putable bonds, and CDS); and credit risk.

George M. Constantinides

Chapter 1

Introduction to Forward and Futures Contracts

Take-Away: Understand the differences between forward and futures contracts institutionally and in terms of the marking-to-market process.

Agenda

- What are derivatives?
- How did derivatives evolve?
- Forward contracts
- Example: Using forward contracts for hedging
- Payoff diagram for long and short forward positions
- Futures contracts
- Example: Using futures contracts for hedging
- Payoff diagram for long and short forward positions
- Other types of derivatives

What are Derivatives?

- *"Textbook" definition:* A derivatives contract is a contract that derives its value from one or more underlying asset prices, reference rates, or indices.
- Because future payoffs of derivatives are determined by future prices of underlying securities, we can derive relationships between the current prices of the derivative and underlying securities based on no-arbitrage arguments.
- The purpose of this book is to develop and study these relationships. We also use these relationships to analyze how derivatives can be used for hedging and speculation.
- These relationships are often independent of factors such as market participants' risk aversion, and of some of the properties of the primitive security itself.
- Derivatives are great devices to . . .

  ➤ Perform successful risk management;
  ➤ Deal with most market frictions;
  ➤ Take on speculative positions;
  ➤ Transfer risk from those who have it to those who want it.

- But proper understanding of the risks and benefits is key to success . . .

  ➤ 1993: Metallgesellschaft losses on oil futures $1.3 billion,
  ➤ 1994: P&G losses on levered swaps ∼$200 million,
  ➤ 1994: Orange County losses on int. rate deriv. ∼$1.5 billion,
  ➤ 1995: Barings Brothers losses on short straddle on futures ∼$1.3 billion,
  ➤ 1998: LTCM losses on convergence strategies ∼$3.5 billion,
  ➤ 2006: Amaranth losses on gas futures ∼$500 million,
  ➤ 2008: Soc. Gen. losses on equity futures ∼$7 billion,
  ➤ 2007–2009 credit crisis: CDSs (credit default swaps) and CDOs (collateralized debt obligations).

How Did Derivatives Evolve?

- Ancient Greek philosopher, Thales, obtained the right to lease the olive oil presses at fixed prices during the harvest.

- Medieval fairs in the 1400s and 1500s involved extensive use of forward contracts on grain and other goods.

- Futures on rice traded in Osaka in the 1700s.

- Options traded in Amsterdam in the 1700s.

- Futures on grains traded in Chicago in 1848 (CBOT).

- Options on equity listed on the CBOT in the 1930s.

- Financial futures traded in Chicago by the 1970s.

Forward Contracts

- A forward contract is an agreement between two parties to buy (sell) something at a pre-specified price on a pre-specified date:
  - ➤ The party agreeing to buy the good in the future is said to *buy a forward,* and has a *long* position.
  - ➤ The party agreeing to sell the good in the future is said to *sell a forward,* and has a *short* position.
- Contract specification:
  - ➤ Amount and quality of good to be delivered;
  - ➤ Delivery price (K);
  - ➤ Time of delivery (T);
  - ➤ Location of delivery.
- The net number of outstanding contracts is always zero:

$$\# \text{ Long Positions} - \# \text{ Short Positions} = 0.$$

- Forward contracts are a *zero-sum game*: The winner's profits equal the loser's losses.

Example: Using Forward Contracts to Hedge Loonies

- An American manufacturer expects to sell one million loonies of its product in Canada and to collect these revenues in six months. The company wants to hedge away its exposure to $/CAD exchange-rate risk.
- The current forward prices for Canadian dollars (expressed in Canadian dollars) are as follows:

Date	Spot	30-day	90-day	180-day
Forward price ($)	0.6597	0.6610	0.6637	0.6681

- To hedge its foreign exchange risk, this manufacturer enters into a forward contract to sell 1M CAD for a price of $0.6681 million in 180 days.
- Two alternative ways to view this transaction:
  (1) The manufacturer commits to converting his CAD revenue into dollars at the pre-agreed rate.
  (2) The manufacturer's profit/loss from her forward contract is $K - S(T)$ dollars on the maturity date T and offsets her foreign-exchange loss/profit. ($S(T)$ is the price of the underlying or "primitive" security on the maturity date.)

- Questions:

  ➢ Doesn't the firm just pass on the risk to someone else?
  ➢ Suppose that the market 180-day CAD forward price appreciates to $0.6781/CAD soon after you sign the forward contract. Has a short position on the forward contract made or lost money?
  ➢ Does the delivery price of the manufacturer's forward contract change over time as the market forward rate fluctuates?

Payoff Diagram for Long and Short Forward Positions

We will often use *payoff diagrams* to represent the cashflow out of a derivative security as a function of the price of the primitive security.

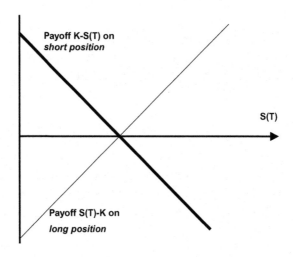

Futures Contracts

- Futures contracts are another type of forward-based derivatives contracts, quite similar to forward contracts, in that they are an agreement between two parties to buy (sell) something at a pre-specified price.
- Whereas forward contracts are generally over-the-counter (OTC) or privately negotiated "deals" between, say, two corporations or a corporation and a bank, futures contracts are:
  - ➤ Exchange-traded and regulated;
  - ➤ Standardized;
  - ➤ Marked to market (*Understand the difference!*)
- Major futures exchanges include the Eurex (jointly operated by Deutsche Borse and SIX Swiss Exchange), CME Group (the merged CME and CBOT), and SGX/SIMEX.
- Standardized terms of the contract usually include:
  - ➤ Amount and quality of good to be delivered.
  - ➤ Time or time span of delivery. The short party usually has a one-month span in which he can deliver.
  - ➤ Delivery location.
  - ➤ Delivery price (K).
  - ➤ Daily price movement and position limits.
- Margin requirements and (typically twice per day) marking-to-market ensure that credit-risk is minimized for the clearing house.
- The initial margin for the EUR/USD contract for EUR 125,000 is about $4000.
- What happened with MF Global?

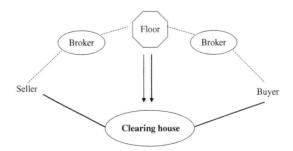

EUR / USD

Example: Using Futures Contracts for Hedging

- From the previous example, if the American firm wants to hedge using a standardized futures contract it would use the JUNE CAD futures contract traded on the IMM (International Money Market — subsidiary of the CME).
- Each contract represents an agreement to purchase 125,000 CAD, so the firm sells eight of these (i.e., agree to sell 1,000,000 CAD). Suppose that the current JUNE futures prices for CAD are:

Date	Spot	MAR	JUNE	SEPT
Futures price ($)	0.6597	0.6631	0.6676	0.6721

- To enter into the futures contract, the firm has to post an *initial margin* of (about)

$$8 \text{ contracts} \times \$1000/\text{contract} = \$8000.$$

- Initial margin acts as a type of performance bond and is set to cover about 99% of anticipated daily price moves. This way, a default by the clearing member to clearing house will not necessarily result in a loss for the clearing house.
- Marking-to-market:
  - ➤ On Day 0, the firm sold the JUNE CAD contracts at a price of $0.6676/CAD.
  - ➤ Suppose on Day 1, the JUNE CAD futures price increases to $0.6690/CAD.
  - ➤ The open position is marked to this new market price and the firm's brokerage account decreases, at the close of Day 1, by

$$(\$0.6690/\text{CAD} - \$0.6676/\text{CAD}) \cdot 1{,}000{,}000 \text{ CAD} = \$1400.$$

  - ➤ The firm now possesses eight short CAD contracts with a futures price of $0.6690/CAD, identical to other JUNE CAD contracts.
  - ➤ The original futures price is no longer a factor in the value of the contracts.

- Maintenance margin:

  ➤ In addition to the initial margin that must be posted before trading, the firm must adhere to a *maintenance margin* requirement on its open position.

  ➤ Maintenance margin is usually 75% of the initial margin, which is $6000 here.

  ➤ After the recent price increase, the firm's margin account now has $6600, which is still higher than the maintenance margin. So the firm will not get a margin call.

  ➤ In the event that the firm's account falls below the maintenance level, a margin call occurs in which the firm must deposit enough funds to bring the account back up to the *initial margin* requirement.

A scenario for the next few days is illustrated below:

Date	JUNE CAD futures price	Gain from short futures position	Add/withdraw to/from margin account	End-of-day margin account
Day 0	0.6676$/CAD		$8000	$8000
Day 1	0.6690$/CAD	−$1400		$6600
Day 2	0.6700$/CAD	−$1000	$2400	$8000
Day 3	0.6685$/CAD	$1500		$9500

This process of margining and marking-to-market (also called "re-settlement") continues until the firm closes out its position by buying eight CAD contracts or delivering 1M CAD at maturity.

CME-traded futures now engage in re-settlements *twice* daily — once to cover price changes in a morning trading session, and again to cover afternoon and overnight risk.

Payoff Diagram for Long and Short Futures Positions

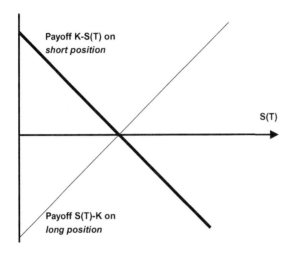

- Although the above diagram is appropriate for many intuitive discussions and even for some numerical calculations, we should note that *the gain or loss from a futures contract is realized gradually, rather than all at once as with a forward.*

Other Types of Derivatives

- Swaps: Essentially portfolios of forward contracts.
- Stock options.
- Stock index options.

Examples: S&P100 options, S&P500 options (CBOE).

- LEAPS.
- Foreign currency options.
- Futures Options (i.e., options on futures).

Contracts with the largest volume and open interest include the T-Bond, S&P500, and the Eurodollar, at the CME.

- Over-the-counter (OTC) options.
- Exotic Options: Bermudan, Asian, look-back, barrier, binary (digital), basket, and *as you like it* options.
- Embedded Option.

Options which are a part of another security, for example, convertible bonds and warrants.

- Swaptions.
- Credit Default Swaps (CDS).
- Collateralized Debt Obligations (CDO).
- Interest Rate Floors, Caps, and Collars.

Chapter 2

Pricing Forwards and Futures

Agenda

- The cost-of-carry model for forward prices without dividends; with fixed dividends; and with proportional continuous dividends or interest
- Carry trades in foreign currency forwards and covered interest parity
- Pricing Treasury Bill forward contracts
- Pricing commodity forward contracts and convenience yield
- Relation between forward and futures prices
- Treasury Bill futures revisited
- Value of forward contract after initiation and the delta
- Value of futures contract after initiation and the delta
- Case study: Metallgesellschaft

The No-Arbitrage Principle

- Chicago versus Harvard MBAs.
- *Arbitrage* as we apply it in class: *A trading strategy that results in a net cash inflow today and has zero probability that we will have a net cash outflow in the future.*
- An equivalent definition of *arbitrage*: Any trading strategy requiring no cash input that has some probability of making profits, with no risk of loss.
- Unlike *equilibrium* rules (e.g., the ICAPM), pricing by the *no-arbitrage principle* require only that there is at least one intelligent investor (hedge funds???) in the economy.
- *Limits of arbitrage*: Investor impatience, a run on the hedge fund, illiquidity, borrowing constraints.

The Cost-of-Carry Model

The Forward Price Equals the Spot Price Plus the Cost-of-Carry

- Items that increase the cost-of-carry:
  - ➤ Interest cost in carrying the spot.
  - ➤ Storage costs, applicable to commodities but irrelevant for financial forward and futures contracts.
- Items that decrease the cost-of-carry:
  - ➤ Interest or dividend earned by the spot.

Arbitrage-free Forward Prices without Dividends

- Suppose you are interested in buying 1 share of IBM stock, which is trading at $100/share. You can either (1) buy it today or (2) commit to buy it in 6 months. Suppose the annualized, continuously compounded risk-free interest rate is 4%. What must the forward price of the stock be?

- If you buy a forward contract today to purchase the share in 6 months, the cost will be $F(t, T)$ in 6 months (t is now and T is 6 months from now).
- If you buy the share today in the spot market, you pay $S(t) = 100$ now.
- In equilibrium, you should be indifferent between the two methods:

$$F(t, T) = S(t) \times e^{r \cdot (T-t)} = \$100 \times e^{0.04 \times 0.5.} = \$102.02$$

$$F(t, T) = \$100 \ (\text{spot}) + \$2.02 \ (\text{cost-of-carry})$$

No-Arbitrage Argument

- Why *must the* forward price be equal to $102.02?
- What if the forward price were $103.00/share?

Table convention: Inflows are positive, outflows are negative.

Transaction	Payoff (at t)	Payoff (at T)
Sell forward	0	103−S(T)
Buy one share	−100	S(T)
Borrow PV(103)	100.96	−103
	0.96	0

- What risk-free rate r should we use here?
- How does the $0.96 profit relate to the discrepancy in the forward price, $103−$102.02 = $0.98?
- What if the forward price were $101.00/share?

Transaction	Payoff (at t)	Payoff (at T)
Buy forward	0	−101 + S(T)
Short one share	100	−S(T)
Lend PV(101)	−99	101
	1	0

Pricing When the Underlying Instrument Pays a Fixed Dividend

- What is the forward price of the stock, if the stock pays a $1 dividend in 3 months? Now if we buy the stock early we capture the dividend

- Two ways of acquiring the IBM share in 6 months:
  - ➢ Use a (long) forward contract and spend $F(t,T)$ **in 6 months** to buy 1 IBM share in 6 months.
  - ➢ Spend PV(1 IBM in 6 months) now to ensure that we have 1 IBM share in 6 months.

  $100 = S(t) = \text{PV}(\$1 \text{ in 3 months}) + \text{PV}(1 \text{ IBM in 6 months})$

The price today for the claim to 1 IBM share in 6 months is

$$100 - \text{PV}(\$1 \text{ in 3 months}).$$

- In equilibrium, we must have

$$F(t,T) = [S(t) - \text{PV}(D)]e^{r(T-t)}$$
$$= \left[100 - 1 \times e^{-0.04 \times 0.25}\right] e^{0.04 \times 0.5} = \$101.01$$

or

$$= \$100 \text{ (spot)} + \$2.02 \text{ (interest cost-of-carry)}$$
$$-\$1.01 \text{ (dividend benefit in holding the spot)}.$$

- Arbitrage argument.

If $F(t,T) = 102 > \$101.01$, then:

Transaction	Payoff at t	Payoff in 3 months	Payoff at T
Sell forward	0		$102-S(T)$
Buy one share	-100	1	$S(T)$
Borrow cash PV(102)	99.98		-102
Borrow PV(D)	0.99	-1	0
	0.97	0	0

If $F(t,T) < 101.01$, then reverse the trades.

Pricing When the Underlying Instrument Pays a Continuous Proportional Dividend

- When we price stock-index and currency forward contracts, we sometimes assume that the dividend or interest:

  (1) is proportional to the price of the asset, and
  (2) is paid continuously.

- **Example**: Consider a 6-month forward contract on the S&P500 Index; the dividend yield (δ) is 3%/year (annualized, c.c.) (i.e., the dividend paid per unit time is equal to δ shares), the index is currently at 1000, and the risk-free rate (annualized, c.c.) is 4%. What is the forward price?

- The "underlying asset" is not one index unit. If we buy the shares in the index today for $1000, and then hold shares and reinvest the dividends proportionally in the shares, at the end of the 6 months we will have $e^{\delta(T-t)} = 1.01511$ shares in the index at the end of six months (Why?).

- The "underlying asset" is $(1.01511)^{-1} = 0.9851$ units of the index.

- If we purchase 0.9851 index units now, it will give us $0.9851 \times 1.01511 = 1$ index unit at the forward's maturity.

- The cost of this (today) is $S(t)e^{-\delta(T-t)} = 1000e^{-0.03 \times 0.5} = \$985.11$.

- This index forward price today is $F(t,T) = 985.11 \times e^{0.4 \times 0.5} = \$1005.01$.

- What should you do to take advantage of the arbitrage opportunity if the index forward price were $1010?

Transaction	Payoff (at t)	Payoff (at T)
Sell forward	0	$1010 - S(T)$
Buy 0.9851 units of the index	$-\$985.10$	$S(T)$
Borrow $985.10	$985.10	$-\$1005$
	0	$5

Or, equivalently, to bring the $5 profit to the present,

Transaction	Payoff (at t)	Payoff (at T)
Sell forward	0	$1010 - S(T)$
Buy 0.9851 units of the index	$-\$985.10$	$S(T)$
Borrow PV(1010)	$990.00	$-\$1010$
	$4.90	0

- Caveats:
  - ➢ Short selling and borrowing may be difficult in some markets.
  - ➢ Also remember that to exploit arbitrage, you need to hold the whole position until maturity and then unwind it all at once — limits of arbitrage.

Pricing Foreign Currency Forwards and Covered Interest Parity

- Pricing foreign currency forwards is very similar to pricing index forwards — a unit of foreign currency can be thought of as *a stock* with a continuous *dividend yield* that is equal to the foreign interest rate.
- **Example**: Assume that the current dollar price of Canadian dollars is $0.67/CAD. The US and Canadian interest rates (annualized, c.c.) are $r = r_{US} = 4\%, \delta = r_{CAD} = 6\%$.
- What is the price today of a Canadian dollar to be delivered in 6 months?

$$F(t,T) = \left[S(t)e^{-\delta(T-t)} \right] \times e^{r(T-t)}$$
$$= S(t)e^{(r-\delta)(T-t)}$$
$$= \$0.67e^{-0.02\times0.5} = \$0.6633/\text{CAD}.$$

- The "underlying asset" of a 6-month CAD forward contract is not 1 CAD today, but rather $e^{-\delta(T-t)}$ CAD today.
- Notice that the CAD interest rate is treated like a continuous proportional dividend paid on the CAD.

- The determination of currency forwards by the cost-of-carry formula is called "covered interest parity".
- How do you take advantage of the violation of the covered interest parity if the forward price of a CAD is \$0.65?

Transaction	Payoff (at t)	Payoff (at T)
Long CAD forward	0	$S(T) - 0.65$
Borrow $e^{-0.06 \times 0.5}$ CAD	$0.67e^{-0.06 \times 0.5}$	$-S(T)$
Sell borrowed CAD and lend the proceeds is USD	$-0.67e^{-0.06 \times 0.5}$	$[0.67e^{-0.06 \times 0.5}] \, e^{0.04 \times 0.5}$ $= \$0.6633$
	0	$\$0.663 - \$.65 = 0.0133 > 0$

- As an exercise, modify the actions in the above table so that we realize a dollar arbitrage profit today instead of realizing \$0.0133 at T (Hint: Modify the dollar amount borrowed today).

Carry Trades

- A carry trade is a speculative strategy of borrowing in a low interest rate currency (dollar, Yen) and investing the proceeds in a high interest rate currency.
- Are carry trades on average profitable? Read the posted document "Profitability of carry trades".
- Consider the carry trade of borrowing in USD and investing in CAD. What is the risk? How may I hedge away the risk?
- Once I hedge away the risk of a carry trade, what is the trade called?

Pricing Treasury Bill Forwards

- **Example**: What is the 4-month (December) forward price for a 3-month T-Bill, assuming that:
  - ➤ The annualized c.c. 4-month interest rate, from August to December (4 months), is 4% and
  - ➤ The annualized c.c. 7-month interest rate, from August to March (7 months), is 5%.

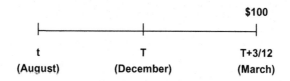

Spot price: $S(t) = 100 \times e^{-0.05 \times \frac{7}{12}} = \$97.13$

Forward price: $F(t, T) = 97.13 \times e^{0.04 \times \frac{4}{12}} = \$98.42$

Pricing Commodity Forward Contracts
with Storage Costs and Convenience Yield

- Most financial assets do not have a *physical* storage cost, whereas most commodities do have.
- Storage costs include the cost of warehousing, transportation, insurance, and spoilage.
- Storage costs *increase* the forward price relative to the spot price.
- If the PV of the storage cost from now to the maturity date is U, we can treat it like a negative, known dividend:

$$F(t, T) = [S(t) + U]e^{r(T-t)}.$$

- In some cases, the storage cost is (1) proportional to the price of the asset, and (2) paid continuously at rate u. The cost of storage can be treated as a negative dividend yield:

$$F(t, T) = \left[S(t)e^{u(T-t)} \right] e^{r(T-t)}.$$

- If $F(t, T) < [S(t) + U]e^{r(T-t)}$ or $F(t, T) = \left[S(t)e^{u(T-t)} \right] e^{r(T-t)}$, is there an arbitrage opportunity? No, because we cannot short a commodity in the spot market.
- *Convenience Yield* is defined to be the "fudge factor" that makes the above relation an equality:

$$F(t, T) = S(t)e^{(r + u - y)(T-t)}.$$

- **Example**: Suppose that the theoretical forward price on a 3-month commodity contract is $S(t)e^{(r+u)(T-t)} = 60$ while the observed forward price is 55. Note that there is no arbitrage opportunity here if we cannot short the commodity in the spot market.
- The convenience yield is defined as:

$$55 = 60 \times e^{-y \times 0.25}.$$

Solve for y:

$$\log(55) = \log(60) - 0.25 \times y$$

$$y = \frac{1}{0.25}[\log(60) - \log(55)] = 0.348, \text{ or } 35\%.$$

- The convenience yield can typically only be positive. If it is negative, there is an arbitrage opportunity.
- For a counter example, we will study Metallgesellschaft.
- The convenience yield for financial forwards is zero.

Summary of Forward Price Formulas

$$F(t, T) = u_t \times e^{r(t,T)(T-t)},$$

where
$F(t,) = $ forward price;
$r(t, T) = $ effective c.c. interest rate between times t and T;
$u_t = $ amount of money needed at t for a strategy that generates one share of the underlying security at T.

Underlying security	u_t
Stock (no dividend)	$S(t)$
Stock with known dividends	$S(t) - \text{PV[dividends]}$
Stock with known dividend yield δ	$S(t)e^{-\delta(T-t)}$
Foreign currency, foreign interest rate δ	$S(t)e^{-\delta(T-t)}$

Relation between Forward and Futures Prices

- Until now we treated forward and futures contracts as essentially equivalent. Now we focus on their differences.
- Definitions: $\widehat{F}_0 : forward\ price$
  $F_0 : futures\ price$
- If the interest rate is zero, the net cashflows of forward and futures contracts are the same.
- **Example**: Consider a long futures contract and a long forward contract on the same spot security, both initiated on day 0 with the same delivery price 340 and 5 days to delivery. Take the following scenario of futures price movement:

Day	Futures price	Cash inflow
0 (opening price on the first day)	340	0
1 (closing price on the first day)	338	-2
2	339	$+1$
3	342	$+3$
4	341	-1
5	343	$+2$
		$+3$

- The net cash inflow for the forward contract is the same as that of the futures contract.
- Since the main difference between a futures and a (otherwise identical) forward is in the timing of cashflows, the two contracts are the same when the interest rate is zero. Then $F_0 = \widehat{F}_0$.

- Repeating the above table in the case of $r = 0$ but now using symbols:

Day	Futures price	Cash inflow
0	F_0	
1	$\tilde{F}_1$	$\tilde{F}_1 - F_0$
2	$\tilde{F}_2$	$\tilde{F}_2 - F_1$
3	$\tilde{F}_3$	$\tilde{F}_3 - F_2$
⋮	⋮	⋮
$T-2$	$\tilde{F}_{T-2}$	$\tilde{F}_{T-2} - \tilde{F}_{T-3}$
$T-1$	$\tilde{F}_{T-1}$	$\tilde{F}_{T-1} - \tilde{F}_{T-2}$
T	$\tilde{F}_T$	$\tilde{F}_T - \tilde{F}_{T-1}$
		$\tilde{F}_T - F_0$
		$= \tilde{S}_T - F_0$

- This shows that, if $r = 0$, holding one long futures contract to maturity generates the same net cashflow as that of an otherwise identical forward contract. Therefore, $F_0 = \hat{F}_0$.

You may skip pages 26–28, if you find them confusing. You are not held responsible for them in the exams.

- We show that $F_0 = \hat{F}_0$ if the interest rate is not zero but **constant**.

- The following futures trading strategy replicates the payoff of an otherwise identical forward:

Day	Contracts	Price	Daily profit	FV factor	Profit at T
0		F_0			
1	$e^{-r(T-1)}$	$\tilde{F}_1$	$e^{-r(T-1)}(\tilde{F}_1 - F_0)$	$e^{r(T-1)}$	$\tilde{F}_1 - F_0$
2	$e^{-r(T-2)}$	$\tilde{F}_2$	$e^{-r(T-2)}(\tilde{F}_2 - F_1)$	$e^{r(T-2)}$	$\tilde{F}_2 - F_1$
3	$e^{-r(T-3)}$	$\tilde{F}_3$	$e^{-r(T-3)}(\tilde{F}_3 - F_2)$	$e^{r(T-3)}$	$\tilde{F}_3 - F_2$
$\vdots$	$\vdots$	$\vdots$	$\vdots$	$\vdots$	$\vdots$
$T-1$	e^{-r}	$\tilde{F}_{T-1}$	$e^{-r}(\tilde{F}_{T-1} - \tilde{F}_{T-2})$	e^r	$\tilde{F}_{T-1} - \tilde{F}_{T-2}$
T	1	$\tilde{F}_T$	$\tilde{F}_T - \tilde{F}_{T-1}$	1	$\tilde{F}_T - \tilde{F}_{T-1}$
					$\tilde{F}_T - F_0$
					$= \tilde{S}_T - F_0$

- Remember:

  Day zero: the opening of the first day;
  Day one: the closing of the first day;
  Day two: the closing of the second day.

- At the end of day 0, we enter into $e^{-r(T-1)}$ futures contracts and hold them for one day.

- At the end of day 1, we close the above position with a net profit of $e^{-r(T-1)}(\tilde{F}_1 - F_0)$, save this profit (or borrow against it if it is negative) in a money market account until day T (which will become $(\tilde{F}_1 - F_0)$ at time T. We then open a new position of $e^{-r(T-2)}$ futures contracts.

- We repeat these steps according to the table until day T.

- Note that, since the time is in units of days here, the interest rate r must be a daily, continuously compounded rate.

- The table will make much more sense once we introduce later on the concept of a **hedge ratio**. Then we will revisit this table.

- Note that if there is a dividend or storage cost associated with the spot our numbers in the table remain unchanged. Why? Because we are not dealing with the spot!

- Now we use the results of the table to show by arbitrage arguments that, if interest rates are known, forward and futures prices must be equal.
- First, the payoff of a forward contract, with a forward price of $\hat{F}_0$, at maturity time T is $\tilde{S}_T - \hat{F}_0$.
- As we showed above, we can replicate a forward time-T cashflow of $\tilde{S}_T - \hat{F}_0$ by employing a trading strategy involving futures contracts that mature at T.
- Since both of the above strategies require no cash input but almost identical cashflows at T, except for the difference between $\hat{F}_0$ and F_0, we must have $\hat{F}_0 = F_0$.
- Otherwise, if $\hat{F}_0 > F_0$ sell a forward and then use futures to replicate a forward, for a total time-T payoff of:

$$(\tilde{S}_T - F_0) - (\tilde{S}_T - \hat{F}_0) = \hat{F}_0 - F_0 > 0.$$

- If $\hat{F}_0 < F_0$, do the opposite, for a profit of $\hat{F}_0 - F_0$.
- Therefore, by arbitrage, F_0 must equal $\hat{F}_0$.
- Are the forward and futures prices equal if there is a dividend or storage cost associated with the spot? Yes, because dividend/storage costs do not enter our argument.
- We can still replicate a forward payoff with futures if the interest rate is known (non-random) but not constant as we have assumed in our example.
- We modify the table as follows: At the **beginning** of day 1, we buy $e^{-r_{1,T}(T-1)}$, where $r_{1,T}$ is the yield rate from the end of day 1 till maturity, and so on.
- What goes wrong with the above proof (that the forward prices equals the future price) when the interest rate is random? We do not know at the **beginning** of Day 1 the yield rate that will prevail from the **end** of Day 1 till maturity.
- When the change in the spot price is fairly uncorrelated with the change in interest rates, $F \approx \hat{F}$ is a good approximation.
- When the change in the spot price is correlated with the change in interest rates, $F \approx \hat{F}$ is a bad approximation.

T-Bond Futures Contract

- If the interest rate unexpectedly increases, the bond price decreases and the future price decreases. At the end of the day when the futures is marked to market, the long pays out cash.
- If the interest rate unexpectedly decreases, the bond price increases and the future price increases. At the end of the day when the futures is marked to market, the long receives cash.
- Thus, the long pays out cash when the interest rate increases and receives cash when the interest rate decreases.
- This is a bad deal for the holder of a long position in a futures contract. Thus the futures contract is less desirable than the forward contract and $F_0 < \hat{F}_0$.
- Later on, we will study Eurodollar futures. In that case, $F_0 > \hat{F}_0$.

Value of a Forward Contract after Initiation and the Hedge Ratio

- Suppose that I have a long 3-month forward contract on a Treasury bond. At the time that I initiated this position, the forward price was 105. Thus the delivery price on my forward contract is $K = 105$. Today (t), the forward price is $\widehat{F} = 108$. What is the value of my forward position?
- I may hedge my position by selling today a forward contract on the T-bond.
- In 3 months (at time T), I receive the T-bond and pay $K = 105$.
- In 3 months, I also deliver the T-bond and receive 108.
- My profit is $\widehat{F} - K = 3$ in 3 months or $3 \times e^{-r \times \frac{3}{13}}$ today.
- In general,

$$\widehat{f} = (\widehat{F} - K)e^{-r(T-t)}.$$

- Does this argument change if the forward contract is a commodity where the cost-of-carry formula does not hold?
- The **forward** price delta of the value of a forward contract is defined as $\partial \widehat{f}/\partial \widehat{F}$. In words, it is the dollar increase (or, decrease) in the value of the forward contract for each $1 increase (or, decrease) in the forward price of the underlying, keeping constant the interest rate.
- The **forward** price delta is

$$\partial \widehat{f}/\partial \widehat{F} = \frac{\partial \left\{ (\widehat{F} - K)e^{-r(T-t)} \right\}}{\partial \widehat{F}} = e^{-r(T-t)}$$

irrespective of whether dividends are paid on the spot or not, this formula applies to both financial and commodity forward contracts.

- For financial forward contracts only and lump sum dividend on the spot, we have $\widehat{F} = [S - \mathrm{PV}(D)]e^{r(T-t)}$.

- The value of the forward position is

$$\widehat{f} = (\{[S-\mathrm{PV}(D)]e^{r(T-t)}\}-K)e^{-r(T-t)} = S-\mathrm{PV}(D)-Ke^{-r(T-t)}.$$

- The spot price delta of the value of a forward contract is defined as $\partial \widehat{f}/\partial S$. In words, it is the dollar increase (or, decrease) in the value of the forward contract for each \$1 increase (or, decrease) in the spot price of the underlying.
- The spot price delta is

$$\frac{\partial \widehat{f}}{\partial S} = \frac{\partial \{S - \mathrm{PV}(D) - Ke^{-r(T-t)}\}}{\partial S} = 1.$$

- For financial forward contracts only and continuous dividend yield on the spot, we have $\widehat{F} = Se^{(r-\delta)(T-t)}$.
- The value of the forward position is

$$\widehat{f} = (Se^{(r-\delta)(T-t)} - K)e^{-r(T-t)} = Se^{-\delta(T-t)} - Ke^{-r(T-t)}.$$

- The spot price delta of the value of a forward contract is

$$\frac{\partial \widehat{f}}{\partial S} = \frac{\partial (Se^{-\delta(T-t)} - Ke^{-r(T-t)})}{\partial S} = e^{-\delta(T-t)}.$$

Value of a Futures Contract after Initiation and the Hedge Ratio

- Suppose that I have a long 3-month futures contract on a Treasury bond. At the time that I initiated this position, the futures price was 105. Thus the delivery price on my futures contract is $K = 105$. Today (t), the futures price is $F = 108$. What is the value of my futures position?
- I may hedge my position by selling today a futures contract on the T-bond.
- At the next marking-to-market, I receive net $F - K = 108 - 105 = 3$. My profit is 3. Notice there is no discounting because the profit or loss is immediate.
- In general,

$$f = F - K.$$

- Does this argument change if the futures contract is a commodity where the cost-of-carry formula does not hold?
- The **futures** price delta of the value of a futures contract is defined as $\partial f / \partial F$. In words, it is the dollar increase (or, decrease) in the value of the futures contract for each \$1 increase (or, decrease) in the futures price of the underlying, keeping constant the interest rate.
- The **futures** price delta is

$$\partial f / \partial F = \frac{\partial (F - K)}{\partial F} = 1.$$

Irrespective of whether dividends are paid on the spot or not, this formula applies to both financial and commodity futures contracts.
- Thus

$$\partial f / \partial F = (\partial \widehat{f} / \partial F) \times e^{r(T-t)}.$$

- For financial futures contracts only and lump sum dividend on the spot, we have $F = [S - \mathrm{PV}(D)]e^{r(T-t)}$.

- The value of the futures position is

$$f = [S - \text{PV}(D)]e^{r(T-t)} - K.$$

- The spot price delta of the value of a futures contract is defined as $\partial f/\partial S$. In words, it is the dollar increase (or, decrease) in the value of the futures contract for each \$1 increase (or, decrease) in the spot price of the underlying.
- The spot price delta is

$$\frac{\partial f}{\partial S} = \frac{\partial\{[S - \text{PV}(D)]e^{r(T-t)} - K\}}{\partial S} = e^{r(T-t)}.$$

- For financial futures contracts only and continuous dividend yield on the spot, we have $F = Se^{(r-\delta)(T-t)}$.
- The value of the futures position is

$$f = Se^{(r-\delta)(T-t)} - K.$$

- The spot price delta of the value of a futures contract is

$$\frac{\partial f}{\partial S} = \frac{\partial(Se^{(r-\delta)(T-t)} - K)}{\partial S} = e^{(r-\delta)(T-t)}.$$

Similarities and Differences between Forward and Futures Contracts (with Known Interest Rate)

- With otherwise identical terms, the forward price is equal to the futures price (if we can legitimately ignore the uncertainty in the interest rate).
- After initiation, however, a futures contract is more volatile than an otherwise identical forward contract, in terms of present values.
- The present-value calculation does not capture a more important difference between the two kinds of contracts. Futures contracts, when used to hedge against an existing position that has payoff at T only, can also create a short-term cashflow problem, if the market fluctuates against the contract holder, while a forward contract does not (Example: Metallgesellschaft).

Metallgesellschaft

- In 1992, MGRM was the US subsidiary of MG AG, or Metallgesellschaft, a German industrial firm.
- The principal creditor and shareholder of MG was Deutsche Bank.
- MGRM sold forward delivery contracts for up to 10 years at fixed prices for petroleum products, including heating oil and gasoline in the central US.
- At the time, MGRM's gross paper profit was about $3 per barrel of crude. MGRM could make such profits on the deals because it was the sole contractor offering the deals.
- Thus, MGRM sold long-dated forward contracts.
- Was it necessary for MGRM to hedge its risk exposure, given its Deutsche Bank connection?
- To hedge its exposure, MGRM bought short-dated NYMEX crude oil and heating oil futures contracts, rolling them over each month. Could MGRM buy long-dated forward contracts? Long-dated futures contracts? Short-dated forward contracts?
- Can we hedge forward contracts with futures contracts?
- **Example**: Suppose that MGRM sold 10 years forward 1 million barrels of oil. Since the hedge ratio of forward contracts is one, if the price of oil increases by $1, MGRM stands to lose $1 million. MGRM hedges the risk by buying N barrels of oil through 1-month futures. Each futures has a hedge ratio of $e^{\frac{1}{12} \times 0.05}$, if the annual interest rate is 5%. If the price of oil increases by $1, MGRM stands to gain $Ne^{\frac{1}{12} \times 0.05}$ million. We pick N such that $Ne^{\frac{1}{12} \times 0.05} = 1$ million. $N = 995{,}842$ barrels.
- *First problem*: The marking-to-market of the futures contracts but not of the forward contracts can cause financial distress.
- In 1993, the spot price of crude oil fell. MGRM made losses on the long positions on the short-dated futures contracts and made equal gains on the short positions on the long-dated forward contracts. Margin calls on the futures positions amounted to $1 billion cash demands on MGRM! MGRM was in financial distress. Why didn't Deutsche Bank help?

- *Second problem*: Basis risk in rolling over the long positions in the futures contracts.
- In this case, MGRM was sometimes buying futures contracts that were overpriced relative to the cost-of-carry formula. How can this happen?
- Why did MGRM not buy gasoline and heating oil (or crude) in the spot market and store it? Huge storage costs.
- Why are these costs not reflected in the cost-of-carry formula for the futures price of crude?
- *Other factors in the MGRM saga*: Plain mistakes in hedging and politics.
- *Epilogue*: In December 1993, the supervisory board of Metallge-sellschaft liquidated both the supply contracts and the futures positions. The losses are estimated between $200 million and $1.3 billion.

Assignment 1

1. A company enters into a short futures contract to sell 5,000 bushels of corn for 200 cents per bushel. The initial margin is $3000 and the maintenance margin is $2000. What price change would lead to a margin call?

2. Consider a portfolio composed of two options written on the same stock:

   - Long a European call option with a strike price K;
   - Short a European put option with a strike price K, with both options maturing at date T.

   (a) What is the payoff of this portfolio at date T (as a function of the time-T stock price)?

   (b) What other derivative has the same type of payoff?

3. After you explain the arbitrage argument behind the interest rate parity (IRP) relation $(F(t,T) = S(t)e^{(r_{US}-r_f)(T-t)})$ to a recruiter, she unexpectedly responds by telling you that this relationship cannot possibly be right: "Look," she says "this relationship implies that when US interest rates rise, the futures price of the yen will increase, meaning that the yen will appreciate in the future. However, we know that an increase in the US interest rate should strengthen the dollar relative to the yen. This can't be right."

   Explain what is wrong with the recruiter's argument.

4. The Intel stock is trading at $100 per share. The risk-free interest rate (annualized, c.c.) is 5.0%. The market assumes that Intel will not pay any dividends within the next 3 months.

   (a) What is the forward price to purchase one share of Intel stock in 3 months?

   (b) Suppose that Intel suddenly announces a dividend of $1 per share in exactly 2 months and assume that the Intel stock price does not change upon the announcement. What is the new 3-month forward price for the Intel stock?

(c) If, after the dividend announcement, the 3-month forward price stays the same, how would you make an arbitrage profit from the market's mispricing?

5. You are running the trading desk at a large, high-grade investment bank. You have the following rates available to you:

Spot Dollar/Yen Exchange Rate	120.44 ¥/$
3-month Forward Dollar/Yen Rate	119.09 ¥/$
1-month USD Risk-free Interest Rate	5.50%
3-month USD Risk-free Interest Rate	6.00%

Assume that there are no transaction costs, and that you can either buy or sell at these exchange rates. In addition, the interest rates above are quoted in annualized, continuously compounded form and are the same for borrowing and lending.

(a) What must the 3-month Japanese (Yen) interest rate (annualized, c.c.) be for there to be no arbitrage?

(b) Suppose that the annualized, continuously compounded 3-month Yen interest rate is 1.0%. Describe exactly what transactions you would undertake at these prices/rates to lock in an arbitrage profit.

Chapter 3

Interest Rate and Currency Swaps

Agenda

- Motivation: Deutsche Telecom largest ever global bond offering
- Plain vanilla interest rate swaps
- Plain vanilla interest rate swap example
- The role of the financial intermediary
- Valuing interest rate swaps
- Hedging the swap
- Plain vanilla foreign currency swaps
- Example: Valuation of foreign currency swap
- Method 1: Present value calculation
- Method 2: Multi-forward contract valuation
- Swaptions
- Eurodollar futures

Introduction

A swap is a financial contract between two counterparties who exchange future cashflows according to a pre-arranged formula. In this chapter, we study the pricing and hedging of the two most important types of swaps: *interest-rate swaps* and *foreign-currency swaps*.

Motivation for Interest Rate and Currency Swaps

Capital Markets Market Flash

Wednesday, June 28, 2000

Deutsche Telekom – Largest Ever Global Bond Offering

Deutsche Telekom (DT) today priced its debut USD 14.5 billion (equivalent) Global Bond issue, a multi-currency offering that included tranches in U.S. dollars, Euros, British pounds sterling and Japanese yen. This landmark transaction is:

- ✓ Largest ever Global bond
- ✓ First ever simultaneous four-currency offering
- ✓ Largest ever corporate bond in the international capital markets
- ✓ Largest ever non-government bond
- ✓ Largest ever fully-integrated E-Bond (electronic order taking and secondary market trading)

- ✓ Largest ever US$ corporate bond
- ✓ Second largest ever fixed-rate € corporate bond
- ✓ Largest ever fixed-rate £ corporate bond
- ✓ Largest ever long-term ¥ bond by a European corporate
- ✓ Deutsche Telekom's Debt IPO: US$, £, and ¥

Issue Summary

The issuer is Deutsche Telekom International Finance B.V., which is unconditionally guaranteed by Deutsche Telekom AG. The ratings of the firm are Aa2/AA- (-watch/-watch). All tranches were Global SEC-registered. Goldman, Sachs & Co., Deutsche Banc Alex. Brown, and Morgan Stanley Dean Witter were joint-lead managers on the issue.

Tranche	Deal Size	Spread (bps)	$Libor
$	**$9.5 bln**		
5yr	$3.0 bln	UST+150 bps	$Libor+49
10yr	$3.0 bln	UST+195 bps	$Libor+73
30yr	$3.5 bln	UST+215 bps	$Libor+95
€	**€3.0 bln**		
5yr	€2.25 bln	Euribor+52 bps	$Libor+56
10yr	€750 mln	Euribor+73 bps	$Libor+77
£	**£925 mln**		
5yr	£625 m	Gilts+145 bps	$Libor+54
30yr	£300 m	Gilts+265 bps	$Libor+131
¥	**¥90 bln**		
5 yr	¥90 bln	¥Libor+25 bps	$Libor+43
Total	**$14.5 bln (equiv.)**		

Rating Sensitive Language

All the securities carry ratings-sensitive coupon language. Specifically, the coupon will step up 50 bps per tranche if *both* Moody's and S&P ratings fall below the single A category (below A3 for Moody's and below A- for S&P). The coupon can step down again if *both* agencies are confirmed above the triple B category (above Baa1 for Moody's and above BBB+ for S&P). This rating sensitive language applies for the life of the notes. Any changes in coupon rates will apply as of the first coupon date after a ratings change that triggers a coupon step-up or step-down.

Marketing/Roadshow

Deutsche Telekom embarked on a high-impact, targeted and extremely well-attended 8-day global roadshow to educate investors about the DT credit story and discuss the European telecommunications landscape. The team from DT included the CFO and Treasurer, who met with investors for the Sterling roadshow for two days in the U.K. (Glasgow, Edinburgh, and London), for the US Dollar roadshow for four days in the U.S. (West Coast, Midwest, New York, and Boston), and for Euros for 2 days in Europe (London, Paris, Amsterdam, Milan, Zurich, Frankfurt). The marketing effort allowed for the transaction to be increased from the original proposed size of $8 billion equivalent.

Order Book Overview

The offering was heavily over-subscribed due in large part to a strong company story, favorable economic conditions, and the appeal of the liquid nature of such an large global debt offering. The final tallies of the order book indicate that over 500 investors bid successfully for a stake in this USD 14.5 billion (equivalent) total debt offering.

Company Overview

With a current market capitalization of €180 billion as of June 28th, 2000 and 1999 revenues of €35.5 billion, DT is the largest telecommunications company in Europe and the third largest in the world.

Plain Vanilla Interest Rate Swaps

- Party A pays Party B interest at a *fixed rate* on Principal "P" for a fixed number of years.
- The principal is *notional*. This means that the principal is used to calculate the interest but is not exchanged by the two parties.
- Party B pays Party A interest at a *floating rate* on principal "P" for a fixed number of years.
- The standard floating rate is either London Interbank Offer Rate (LIBOR), the rate at which a bank is willing to lend to another bank; or, the T-Bill rate.
- Motivation: Why would Deutsche Telecom wish to trade in interest rate swaps after its global bond offering?
- Like forward contracts, swap contracts normally have zero value (i.e., they are signed without payment) at initiation.
- Following the Dodd–Frank Act, in 2014, all swaps are gradually moving to a system where they are cleared by a clearing corporation and are marked to market on a daily basis.

Plain Vanilla Interest Rate Swap Example

- Firms A and B have the following borrowing rates available to them:

	Fixed (%)	Floating
Firm A	10.0	6-month LIBOR + 0.30%
Firm B	11.2	6-month LIBOR + 1.00%

- Party A has an *absolute* advantage in both markets. Possible reasons: A may have better credit rating or better banking relationships than B.
- Absolute advantage is not what motivates the swap. As we shall see below, it is the *comparative* advantage that motivates the swap.
- If A borrows at the fixed rate (10%) and B borrows at the variable rate (LIBOR plus 1%), the total cost is 11% plus LIBOR.
- If A borrows at the variable rate (LIBOR plus 0.3%) and B borrows at the fixed rate (11.2%), the total cost is 11.5% plus LIBOR.

- The difference between 11.5% plus LIBOR and 11% plus LIBOR is 0.5%. We call this difference the *comparative* advantage.
- Since A pays 1.2% less in fixed-rate borrowing and 0.7% less in floating-rate borrowing, A has a *comparative* advantage in the fixed-rate market and B has a comparative advantage in the floating-rate market.
- If A wants to borrow $10 million floating and B wants to borrow $10 million fixed, how can each borrow in her/his comparative-advantage market and then carry out an advantageous swap?

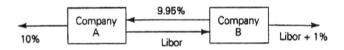

- A effectively pays LIBOR + 0.05%, 0.25% less than it would pay by borrowing directly at floating rate.
- B effectively pays 10.95% fixed, 0.25% less than it would pay by borrowing directly at fixed rate.
- The net gain to the two borrowers is 50 bps, which is exactly equal to the size of the comparative advantage.
- In this example, the 50 bps are split evenly between the two parties. In reality, it is the competition among swap dealers that determines the split.
- Note 1 bp or "one basis point" is 0.01%. One hundred bps is 1%.

The Role of the Financial Intermediary

- Usually, parties A and B do not enter into a swap on their own. (You don't buy apples from an apple farmer either.) Each party calls a number of swap dealers in financial institutions and shops around for the best rate. Swap dealers act as intermediaries between firms.

- In this example, the swap dealer at the bank earns 10 bps and each of the two firms gets a 20 bps improvement in their borrowing rate. Again, in reality, it is the competition among swap dealers that determines the split.
- In typical interest-rate swaps, the size of a bank's profit is 2–3 bps because there is a lot of competition.
- The bank either has offsetting swaps, as shown here, or hedges any "warehoused" swaps.
- The bank bears all of the default risk that comes with the swap.

Valuing Interest Rate Swaps

- **Example**: Consider a plain vanilla 2-year interest-rate swap of a fixed rate against the 6-month LIBOR rate with a notional amount of $1 million.
- The $1 million principal is *notional*. The principal is used to calculate the interest but is not exchanged by the two parties.
- The floating LIBOR rate to be paid on each future payment date is usually set according to the market floating rate 6 months prior to the payment date.
- If the 6-month LIBOR rate in 12 months is 8%, then the floating-rate payer pays $0.5 \times 8\% \times \$1\,\mathrm{M}$ in 18 months.
- The first floating-rate payment (in 6 months) is known at initiation — it is the current 6-month LIBOR rate.
- C denotes the fixed rate of the swap.
- $\tilde{R}(t, t')$ denotes the time-t market LIBOR rate for borrowing from t to t', with both rates annualized (with semi-annual compounding).
- Table of cashflows (in millions):

Date (months)	6	12	18	24
Fixed rate	$C/2$	$C/2$	$C/2$	$C/2$
Floating rate	$\dfrac{R(0,6)}{2}$	$\dfrac{\tilde{R}(6,12)}{2}$	$\dfrac{\tilde{R}(12,18)}{2}$	$\dfrac{\tilde{R}(18,24)}{2}$

- In the *present-value approach* to valuing the interest-rate swap, we apply the following trick. We add $1 million to the cashflows in 24 months of the party receiving the fixed rate and to the party receiving the variable rate.
- Since the $1 million exchange is a wash, the two swap counterparties remain indifferent.
- The swap cashflows now look as follows:

Date (months)	6	12	18	24
Fixed rate	$C/2$	$C/2$	$C/2$	$(C/2) + 1$
Floating rate	$\dfrac{R(0,6)}{2}$	$\dfrac{\tilde{R}(6,12)}{2}$	$\dfrac{\tilde{R}(12,18)}{2}$	$\dfrac{\tilde{R}(18,24)}{2} + 1$

- The cashflows of the floating rate side are identical to the cashflows of a floating-coupon bond. But a floating-coupon bond sells at par at the time of issue. Therefore, the present value of the cashflows of the floating rate side is 1.
- To elaborate: I can replicate the cashflows of the floating-coupon bond by investing \$1 million at the LIBOR rate and keep rolling the principal every 6 months. Since I can achieve these cashflows with a \$1 million investment, the value of these cashflows is \$1 million.
- Now we need to find the present value of the fixed cashflows.
- Suppose that the term structure for the LIBOR rate (annualized, semiannual compounding) is given by

Maturity	6 months	12 months	18 months	24 months
LIBOR	6%	6.3%	6.7%	7%

- The present value of the fixed cashflows is

$$\frac{C/2}{1+0.06/2} + \frac{C/2}{(1+0.063/2)^2} + \frac{C/2}{(1+0.067/2)^3} + \frac{1+C/2}{(1+0.07/2)^4}.$$

- The value of the swap is the difference between the PV of a floating-coupon bond and the PV of a fixed-coupon bond:

$$1 - \frac{C/2}{1+0.06/2} - \frac{C/2}{(1+0.063/2)^2} - \frac{C/2}{(1+0.067/2)^3} - \frac{1+C/2}{(1+0.07/2)^4}.$$

- At initiation, the *market term rate*, C, is set such that the value of the swap is zero:

$$1 - \frac{C/2}{1+0.06/2} - \frac{C/2}{(1+0.063/2)^2} - \frac{C/2}{(1+0.067/2)^3}$$
$$- \frac{1+C/2}{(1+0.07/2)^4} = 0.$$

- Rearrange the equation as follows:

$$1 - \frac{1}{(1+0.07/2)^4} = C \times \left[\frac{1/2}{1+0.06/2} + \frac{1/2}{(1+0.063/2)^2} \right.$$

$$\left. + \frac{1/2}{(1+0.067/2)^3} + \frac{1/2}{(1+0.07/2)^4} \right]$$

We solve for the market rate as $C = 0.0697$ or 6.97%.

- If the 2-year yield on a Treasury Note is 6.95%, the swap market rate is quoted as TN + 2 bps because 6.95% + 2 bps = 6.97%.
- An interest-rate swap can also be thought of as a series of forward contracts, with each forward contract involving the exchange of a fixed-rate payment with a floating-rate payment. A swap's value is the total value of all the component forward contracts.
- For plain vanilla interest-rate swaps, the illustrated present-value calculation is the simplest way to find the value of the swap.

Hedging the Swap

- In practice, interest-rate swaps are hedged by using *Eurodollar Futures* (Hull, pp. 137–141, McDonald 5.7) and *Forward Rate Agreements* (FRAs, Hull, pp. 86–89). We talk about Eurodollar futures at the end of this note.

- Below, we illustrate how to use the LIBOR market (or discount bonds) to hedge a scheduled floating payment $\$1 \times \tilde{R}(6,12)/2$ million that we make in 12 months.

  (1) At time 0, we invest $B(0,6) = \frac{1}{1+R(0,6)/2}$ million at the 6-month LIBOR rate for 6 months. In 6 months, we receive $\$1$ million. We roll it over for another 6 months at the prevailing LIBOR rate $\tilde{R}(6,12)$. Six months later, we receive $1 + \tilde{R}(6,12)/2$.

  (2) At time 0, we also borrow $B(0,12) = \frac{1}{1+R(0,12)}$ million for 12 months at the 12-month LIBOR rate $R(0,12)$, annually compounded. Twelve months later, we repay it at a cost of $\$1$ million.

- By spending $B(0,6) - B(0,12)$ million now, we generate the net inflow $\frac{\tilde{R}(6,12)}{2}$ million in 12 months to make our floating payment of $\frac{\tilde{R}(6,12)}{2}$ million.

Plain Vanilla Foreign Currency Swaps

- A foreign currency swap is usually used to transform a loan in a foreign currency into a domestic-currency loan; or, the converse.
- Why would Deutsche Telecom wish to trade in foreign currency swaps after its global bond offering?
- **Example**: IBM and British Petroleum (BP) have the following borrowing rates available to them in dollars and sterling:

	Dollars	Sterling
IBM	8.0%	11.6%
BP	10.0%	12.0%

- Assume for simplicity that the spot exchange rate is 1.5 USD/GBP.
- Total interest in the "bad" borrowing combination:
  - If BP borrows $15 million at 10% interest, in the first year, it pays interest $1.5 million.
  - If IBM borrows sterling 10 million at 11.6%, in the first year, it pays interest sterling 1.16 million or $1.74 million.
- BP and IBM pay total interest $3.24 million in the first year.
- Total interest in the "good" borrowing combination:
  - If IBM borrows $15 million at 8% interest, in the first year, it pays interest $1.2 million.
  - If BP borrows Sterling 10 million at 12%, in the first year, it pays interest Sterling 1.2 million or $1.8 million.
  - BP and IBM pay total interest $3.0 million in the first year.
- IBM has a comparative advantage borrowing dollars, BP has a comparative advantage borrowing sterling. The comparative advantage is $3.24 − $3.0 = $0.24 million in interest in just the first year.

- Suppose that IBM needs to borrow £10 million sterling and BP $15 million dollars. Then they can undertake the following currency swap:

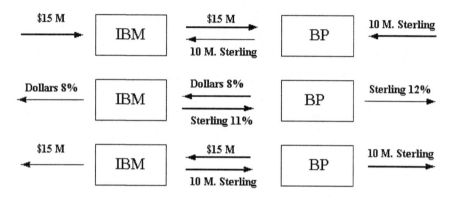

- A financial intermediary can help out by taking on the foreign-currency risk

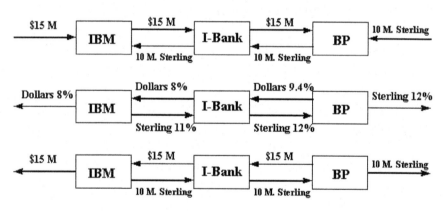

- The 9.4% and 11% rates are set by competition amongst dealers.
- In foreign currency swaps, the principal is actually swapped at initiation and at maturity. Contrast this with interest rate swaps where the principal is notional.
- The financial institution hedges away its currency risk by using forward or futures contracts.

Example: Valuation of a Foreign Currency Swap

- The term structure in both the US and Japan is flat, and continuously-compounded risk-free rates are $r_J = 4\%$ in Japan and $r_{US} = 9\%$ in US. A bank is in a swap where each year it pays 8%/year in dollars and receives 5%/year in yen. The principal amounts in the two currencies are $10 million and $1200 million yen. The swap is past initiation and there are three years to the swap maturity. The current exchange rate is 110 yen/dollar. Value the remainder of the swap.
- Swap parameters:
  - ➤ Principal amounts: $P_{US} = \$10\,M$, $P_J = 1200\,M$ Yen.
  - ➤ Swap coupon rates: $c_{US} = 8\%, c_J = 5\%$.
- Market interest rates: $r_{US} = 9\%, r_J = 4\%$.
- Spot exchange rate: 110 yen/dollar or equivalently, 0.0091 dollars/yen.

Method 1: Present-Value Calculation
of the Value of the Swap

- The remainder of the swap is an exchange of two bonds:

$$B_{\text{US}} = c_{\text{US}}P_{\text{US}}e^{-r_{\text{US}} \times 1} + c_{\text{US}}P_{\text{US}}e^{-r_{\text{US}} \times 2}$$

$$+ (c_{\text{US}}P_{\text{US}} + P_{\text{US}})e^{-r_{\text{US}} \times 3}$$

$$= 0.08 \times 10 \times e^{-0.09 \times 1} + 0.08 \times 10 \times e^{-0.09 \times 2}$$

$$+ (0.08 \times 10 + 10) \times e^{-0.09 \times 3}$$

$$= \$9.64 \text{ million},$$

$$B_{\text{J}} = c_{\text{J}}P_{\text{J}}e^{-r_{\text{J}} \times 1} + c_{\text{J}}P_{\text{J}}e^{-r_{\text{J}} \times 2} + (c_{\text{J}}P_{\text{J}} + P_{\text{J}})e^{-r_{\text{J}} \times 3}$$

$$= 0.05 \times 1200 \times e^{-0.04 \times 1} + 0.05 \times 1200 \times e^{-0.04 \times 2}$$

$$+ (0.05 \times 1200 + 1200) \times e^{-0.04 \times 3}$$

$$= 1230.55 \text{ million yen.}$$

The value of the swap to the bank is

$$\frac{1230.55}{110} - 9.64 = \$1.55 \text{ million.}$$

- Consider the following variation to the example. Suppose that the swap were initiated today. What, if any, side payment needs to be made?

  — The value to the bank of the initial exchange is: $10 − 1200/110 = −\$0.909$ million.
  — The value to the bank of the swap after the initial exchange was earlier calculated to be $1.55 million.
  — The net value to the bank at initiation is $1.55 − \$0.909 = \$0.641$ million. The bank needs to make a side payment of $0.641 million at initiation.

Method 2: Multi-Forward-Contract Calculation of the value of the Swap

- This method illustrates how, in practice, we use information from the forward price, $\widehat{F}_t$, to calculate the value of the forward contract.
- From the perspective of the bank, the remainder of this swap is composed of three foreign currency forward contracts.
- (1) A 1-year long position in a forward contract (past initiation) for the delivery of 0.05×1200 m $= 60$ million yen with delivery price $K = 0.08 \times 10$ m $= 0.8$ million dollars.
- (2) A 2-year long position in a forward contract for the delivery of 60 million yen with delivery price 0.8 million dollars.
- (3) A 3-year long position in a forward contract for the delivery of $60 + 1200 = 1260$ million yen with delivery price $0.8 + 10 = 10.8$ million dollars.
- The value of the swap is the sum of the values of the three forward contracts.
- We illustrate how we value the 1-year forward position:

  ➤ Suppose that the 1-year forward exchange rate is 104.64 yen/dollar or, equivalently, 0.0096 dollars/yen (verify on your own that this exchange rate is consistent with covered interest rate parity).
  ➤ Convert the 60 million yen to be delivered in one year into $60/104.64$ million dollars to be delivered in one year.
  ➤ Convert the $60/104.64$ million dollars to be delivered in one year into $[60/104.64]e^{-0.09 \times 1}$ million dollars today, where the US interest rate is 9%.
  ➤ The value of the 1-year forward position is $[60/104.64 - 0.8]e^{-0.09 \times 1}$ million dollars.

- By contrast, by the present-value method (method 1), we converted the 60 million yen to be delivered in one year into $60 \times e^{-r_{yen}(T-t)}$ yen today; and then converted the yen into dollars today using the spot exchange rate.
- We illustrated how we value the 1-year forward position. As an exercise, use the 2-year forward rate (consistent with covered interest rate parity) to value the 2-year forward position.
- Use the 3-year forward rate (consistent with covered interest rate parity) to value the 3-year forward position.
- Convince yourself that the two methods give the same answer, if covered interest rate parity holds.

Swaptions

- A swaption gives the buyer the right, *but not the obligation*, to enter into a certain swap at a certain time in the future at pre-specified terms.
- For example, an interest-rate swaption would give its owner the right to enter, in 6 months, into a 5-year swap in which she would receive LIBOR rate on $10 million in exchange for a fixed rate of 5.5% on $10 million.
- The swaption gains in value and is likely to be exercised in 6 months if the 5-year bond yield increases relative to the LIBOR rate.

Credit Default Swaps (CDSs)

- A CDS on a bond is an insurance contract. If you buy a CDS on a corporate bond of par value $100 and the bond defaults and pays you only $60, your counterparty in the CDS pays you the difference: $100 − $60 = $40.
- Why did AIG sell huge amounts of CDSs on mortgage-backed securities?
- We will price CDSs later on in the course when we introduce the Merton model.
- Fun reading: Michael Lewis' "The Big Short".

Eurodollar Futures

- Very liquid contracts on the CME and other exchanges.
- Widely used to hedge interest rate swaps. In fact they were custom-made for this purpose.
- The underlying is the 3-month LIBOR rate.
- Contract maturities are in March, June, September, December, up to 10 years.
- **Example**: let the futures price of the September contract on the CME be 96.80.
- The implied futures annualized interest is $R = 100 - 96.80 = 3.20\%$, quarterly compounded.
- By the end of September, the long side to this contract receives cumulatively (through the daily marking-to-market)

$$\$1 \text{ million} \times \frac{1}{4} \left[\frac{3.20}{100} - \frac{L}{100} \right],$$

where L is the September prevailing 3-month LIBOR rate.
- One day after you bought the Eurodollar futures, the futures price drops by one bp: from 96.80 to 96.79. Show that through the marking-to-market, you lose $25.
- **Interpretation**

  ➤ The long in this contract effectively locks in the annualized interest of 3.20%, quarterly compounded, on a notional lending of $1 million principal.

  ➤ The margin on such a big bet with one contract is merely $1000! Thus the leverage is high.

  ➤ What other contract can you use to lock in the interest of 3.20%, quarterly compounded, on a notional lending of $1 million principal?

- **Hedging a swap with Eurodollar futures**: Suppose that in September we expect to receive LIBOR on an interest rate swap with notional $1 million. How do we hedge it? Do we buy or sell Eurodollar futures? How many contracts? Which maturity?

- What happened to this market now that the interest rates are close to zero? Selling pickles . . .

Eurodollar Futures versus Forward Rates

- Now we address differences between the Eurodollar forward and futures rates. If in September, the prevailing LIBOR rate exceeds 3.20%, the long future loses money on the contract because she essentially committed to lend her money at 3.20%.
- Through the marking-to-market, when the LIBOR rate increases, the long in the futures contract loses money; and when the LIBOR rate decreases, the long in the futures contract makes money. Thus the futures is less desirable than the forward contract.
- To entice someone to buy the Eurodollar futures, the futures rate of 3.20% is higher than the forward interest rate.
- Equivalently, by observing this traded futures contract on the CME, we infer that the forward interest rate is *lower* than 3.20%.
- Therefore, the forward *price* is greater than $100 - 3.20$.

Assignment 2

1. Companies A and B have been offered the following rates per annum on a $10 million five-year loan:

	Fixed rate	Floating rate
Company A	12.0%	LIBOR + 0.1%
Company B	13.4%	LIBOR + 0.6%

Company A requires a floating-rate loan; company B requires a fixed-rate loan. Design a swap that will net a bank, acting as intermediary, 10 basis points per annum and appear to be equally attractive to both companies.

2. Company X wishes to borrow US dollars (USD) at a fixed rate of interest. Company Y wishes to borrow Japanese Yen (JPY) at a fixed rate of interest. The amounts required by the two companies are roughly the same at the current exchange rate. The companies have been quoted the following interest rate (annualized, simple) at which they can borrow in JPY and USD:

	Yen	Dollars
Company X	4.0%	8.0%
Company Y	5.5%	8.4%

Design a swap that will net a bank, acting as intermediary, 50 basis points per annum. Make the swap equally attractive to the two companies and ensure that the bank assumes all foreign exchange risk.

3. On page 39 of Chapter 3, we showed that a cashflow of the random amount $\tilde{R}(6, 12)/2$ in 12 months has a present value of B $(0, 6)$–B $(0, 12)$. Let us denote the *forward* interest rate (annualized, semiannual compounding) by $R_f(6, 12)$. Using an argument that is similar to the earlier one (or using any other argument that

you like), prove that the present value of a cashflow $R_f(6, 12)/2$ in 12 months is B(0, 6)-B(0, 12), which is exactly the PV of a cashflow of $\tilde{R}(6, 12)/2$ in 12 months.

4. (*Interest Rate Swap Pricing*) Suppose that the LIBOR rates (annualized, semiannual compounding) for maturities up to 2 years are given by

Maturity	6 months	12 months	18 months	24 months
LIBOR	6%	6.2%	6.4%	6.6%

(a) What is the market fixed rate (annualized, semiannual compounding) for a two-year fixed-floating swap with semiannual payments in which the floating rate at the end of each six-month period is the six-month LIBOR rate at the beginning of the period?

(b) XYZ entered into such a swap, as the fixed-rate payer, with a notional amount of $10 million. Two months later, suppose that the market LIBOR rate term structure becomes flat and equal to 6% (annualized, continuous compounding) for all maturities. What is the value of the swap to XYZ?

(c) Consider a new swap that is the same as the swap in part (a), except that the floating rate in the new swap is (10% — LIBOR) (annualized, semiannual compounding). Using the result from step (a), calculate the market swap rate for this new swap. (*Hint*: You do not need to know how to do Step (a) to answer this question.)

(d) Consider, again, the same swap in Step (a) and assume that the fixed rate of the swap is the market swap rate that you have calculated in Step (a). Suppose that the swap now has a new feature that will terminate the swap contract (without any party being compensated) whenever the floating 6-month LIBOR rate reaches above 7.5% before maturity. Without making any numerical calculations, do you expect the new swap to have positive, zero, or negative value to the fixed-rate payer? (Note: You do not need to know how to do step (a) to answer this question.)

5. (*Foreign currency swap pricing*) The term structure in both the euros and USD is flat and the continuously compounded risk-free rates are $r_{USD} = 6\%$ and $r_{EUR} = 4\%$. You are interested in entering into a three-year currency swap in which each year you pay 3% per year in euros. The principal amounts in the two currencies are 10 million euros and $15 million. The current exchange rate is 0.6600 EUR/USD.

(a) What is the market USD coupon rate for this swap?

(b) Six months after entering into this swap, the market exchange rate becomes 0.64 EUR/USD. What is the value of the swap contract to you? What is the value of the swap contract to the counterparty of the swap?

Chapter 4

Introduction to Options and No-Arbitrage Restrictions

Agenda

- Basic types of options
- Profit diagrams for options at maturity
- Cashflow or payoff diagrams at maturity
- The Chicago Board Options Exchange
- Notation
- No-arbitrage bounds on option prices
- No-arbitrage bounds for options on stocks without dividends
- European put-call parity for stocks without dividends
- European put-call parity for stocks with dividends
- American put-call parity for stocks with dividends
- Summary

Basic Types of Options

- A *call option* gives its owner the right (but not the obligation) to buy an asset at a fixed price (the *exercise* or *strike* price).
- A *put* option gives its owner the right (but not the obligation) to sell an asset at a fixed price.
- *European* option: The holder can exercise it only at maturity (expiration).
- *American* option: The holder can exercise it at any time up to and including maturity.
- *Pin risk*: The uncertainty faced by an option *writer* as to whether the option *buyer* will decide to exercise the option.
- The *intrinsic value* of an option is its value if exercised immediately.
- The *moneyness* of an option refers to whether the option's intrinsic value is positive, zero, or negative.
- Definitions of *in-the-money* (ITM), *out-of-the-money* (OTM) and *at-the-money* (ATM) calls and puts:

	$S < K$	$S = K$	$S > K$
Call	OTM	ATM	ITM
Put	ITM	ATM	OTM

Profit Diagrams for Options at Maturity

- The *profit* to the long or short at the option's maturity is defined as the payoff net of the premium. The premium is denoted by C for the call and P for the put.
- We often depict the profit as a function of the underlying asset price at maturity, $S(T)$.

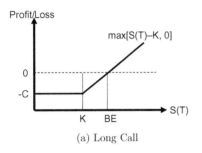

(a) Long Call

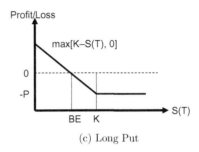

(c) Long Put

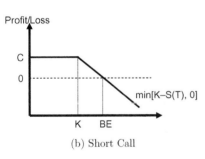

(b) Short Call

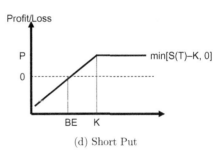

(d) Short Put

- The owner of the option *breaks even* only when the intrinsic value is at least enough to cover the premium paid.
- Break-even points in the payoff diagrams are labeled BE.

Cashflow or Payoff Diagrams at Maturity

- The value of an option at maturity is represented by *payoff* or *cashflow* diagrams.
- These are essentially the same as profit or value diagrams. The only difference is that the maturity payoff is now shown *gross*, so that premium paid is not subtracted out.

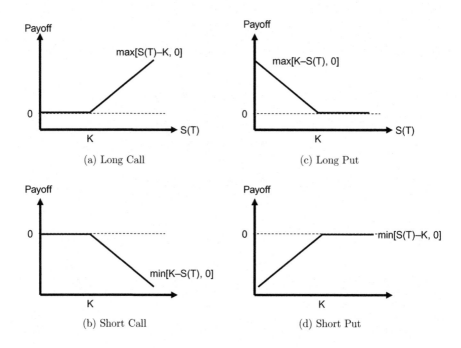

(a) Long Call

(c) Long Put

(b) Short Call

(d) Short Put

- The long option payoff is always positive. A long option position thus is a *limited liability* transaction. Unlike forward-based derivatives, you cannot lose more than your premium outlay.

The Chicago Board Options Exchange (CBOE)

The CBOE is the world's largest options exchange by value of trades.

- Stock options on the CBOE:

  ➤ A contract represents 100 shares.
  ➤ American-style.
  ➤ Maturity is on the Saturday following the third Friday of the contract month.
  ➤ Maturity dates are based on a January, February, or March expiration cycle:

Cycle	Cycle months	Firms on cycle
January	1 4 7 10	IBM, Intel
February	2 5 8 11	Coke, Dell
March	3 6 9 12	Philip Morris, Ford

  ➤ Options are traded in the two closest months and the subsequent two months of the cycle.
  ➤ Options are not protected for cash dividends. An exception is sometimes made for dividends larger than 10%, at the discretion of a committee of the Options Clearing Corporation. In that case, the call writer is required to deliver the dividend along with the stock, if the call writer is "assigned".
  ➤ The options *are* adjusted for stock splits and stock dividends. A 20% stock dividend is the same as a 6-for-5 stock split. After an n-*for*-m stock split, the exercise price is reduced to m/n of its previous value and the number of shares represented by a contract is increased by a factor of n/m.

- All index options are European, including the S&P 100 Index option (XEO). There is also the S&P 100 Index option (OEX) which is American.

- In addition to the above options that expire at the end of a month, we now have options that expire at the end of a week. Who uses them?
- Options on futures are listed on futures exchanges.

Notation

Current date	t
Maturity or expiration date	T
Price of the *underlying* asset	$S(t)$
Current price of a \$1 face-value bond that matures at T	$B(t,T)$, or $e^{-r(T-t)}$
Exercise (strike) price	K
Value of a European call	$c(S,K,t,T)$
Value of an American call	$C(S,K,t,T)$
Value of a European put	$p(S,K,t,T)$
Value of an American put	$P(S,K,t,T)$

No-Arbitrage Bounds for Options

The following restrictions hold regardless of whether the underlying stock pays dividends or not. Prove them on your own by showing that there exists an arbitrage opportunity, if these restrictions are violated.

- A call is never worth more than the stock:

$$C(S, K, t, T) \leq S(t), \quad c(S, K, t, T) \leq S(t).$$

- A put is never worth more than the exercise price:

$$P(S, K, t, T) \leq K, \quad p(S, K, t, T) \leq K.$$

- European puts are never worth more than the present value of the exercise price:

$$p(S, K, t, T) \leq K \cdot B(t, T) < K.$$

Intuitively, this has to hold since the time-T payoff to a European put holder is bounded (from above) by K.

- American options are at least as valuable as their European counterparts:

$$C(S, K, t, T) \geq c(S, K, t, T),$$
$$P(S, K, t, T) \geq p(S, K, t, T).$$

- American options with more time to maturity are at least as valuable; i.e., for $T_2 > T_1$,

$$C(S, K, t, T_2) \geq C(S, K, t, T_1),$$
$$P(S, K, t, T_2) \geq P(S, K, t, T_1).$$

Note: These do not always hold for European options.

- An American option is worth at least its exercised value:

$$C(S, K, t, T) \geq \max\left[0, S(t) - K\right],$$
$$P(S, K, t, T) \geq \max\left[0, K - S(t)\right].$$

- **Example**: Do we have an arbitrage opportunity if, for Intel stock with $S(t) = \$100$, a call option with $K = \$90$ and 6 months to maturity is trading at $9? Yes. How?

Note: This rule does not always hold for European options. Think of dividends and early exercise.

No-Arbitrage Bounds for Options on Stocks Without Dividends

- For a stock that does not pay dividends:

$$c(S, K, t, T) \geq \max\left[0, S(t) - K \cdot B(t, T)\right],$$
$$C(S, K, t, T) \geq \max\left[0, S(t) - K \cdot B(t, T)\right].$$

- **Example:** Do we have an arbitrage opportunity if, for Intel stock with $S(t) = \$100$, a call option with $K = \$90$ and 6 months to maturity is trading at $11? Assume that *Intel* will not pay dividend within the next 6 months and the interest rate (c.c., annualized) is 10%. Is there an arbitrage?

Yes, because $S(t) - K \cdot B(t, T) = 100 - 90e^{-0.5 \times 0.10} = 14.4$ and $11 < 14.4$. How?

		Payoff at T	
Transaction	Payoff at t	If $S(T) \leq 90$	If $S(T) > 90$
Buy one call	-11	$0 S(T)$	-90
Short one share	100	$-S(T)$	$-S(T)$
Lend	$-K \cdot B = -85.6$	90	90
NET	3.4	≥ 0	0

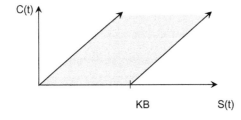

- Also for a stock that does not pay dividends:

$$P(S, K, t, T) \geq p(S, K, t, T) \geq \max\left[0, K \cdot B - S\right].$$

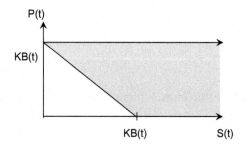

European Put-Call Parity for Stocks Without Dividends

- For European options on non-dividend paying stocks

$$c(S, K, t, T) - p(S, K, t, T) = S(t) - \text{PV}(K).$$

Intuition: A certain portfolio of options has the same payoff at maturity as a share of stock and bonds, so the two portfolios must have the same initial price. If this relation does not hold, there is an arbitrage opportunity.

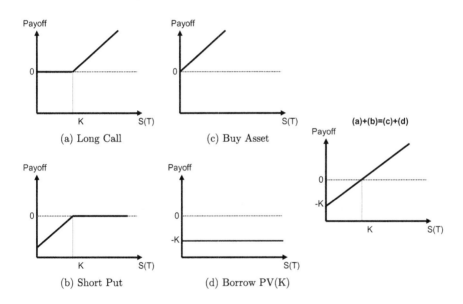

(a) Long Call   (c) Buy Asset

(b) Short Put   (d) Borrow PV(K)

- **Example:** $K = 50, S = 50, r = 5\%$ annual c.c., $T - t = 1$ month, $c = 4.5$, $p = 4.0$.
  Since $c - p + K \cdot B = 4.5 - 4 + 50 \times e^{-0.05 \times \frac{1}{12}} = 50.29 > S$, the put-call parity is violated and the stock is relatively underpriced. Therefore, we buy one share of the underpriced stock and hedge it.

		Final (T) cashflow	
Transaction	**Initial (t) cashflow**	**$S(T) < 50$**	**$S(T) > 50$**
Buy one share	$-\$50$	$S(T)$	$S(T)$
Write one call	$\$4.5$	0	$-[S(T) - \$50]$
Buy one put	$-\$4.0$	$\$50 - S(T)$	0
Borrow	$\$49.79$	$-\$50$	$-\$50$
Net	$\$0.29$	0	0

- If $c - p + \mathrm{PV}(K) < S$, then reverse all the actions in the table.
- There are four different ways to interpret the actions taken in the table:

  ➤ We bought one share and hedged it by synthetically shorting one share by (1) writing a call, (2) buying a put, and (3) borrowing the present value of the strike.

  ➤ We wrote a call and hedged it by synthetically buying a call by (1) buying one share, (2) buying a put, and (3) borrowing the present value of the strike.

  ➤ We bought one put and hedged it by synthetically writing a put by (1) buying one share, (2) writing a call, and (3) borrowing the present value of the strike.

  ➤ We borrowed the present value off the strike and hedged it by synthetically lending the present value off the strike by (1) buying one share, (2) writing a call, and (3) buying a put.

- The most important interpretation of the put-call parity relation $c - p = S - \mathrm{PV}(K)$ is:

A long call and a short put with common expiration date and strike are equivalent to a forward position on the underlying past initiation with delivery price equal to the strike price K and delivery time the expiration date of the options, independent of dividends on the stock.

European Put-Call Parity for Stocks With Dividends

- Since the payoff of a long European call and short European put equals the payoff of a long forward position past initiation, we have:

$$c(S, K, t, T) - p(S, K, t, T) = [S(t) - \text{PV}(D)] - \text{PV}(K)$$

for lump-sum dividend or

$$c(S, K, t, T) - p(S, K, t, T) = \left[S(t)e^{-\delta(T-t)} \right] - \text{PV}(K)$$

for continuous dividend yield δ.

- Show as an exercise that violation of these restrictions leads to arbitrage profits.

American Put-Call Parity for Stocks
With Dividends

- For *American* calls and puts on dividend paying stocks, the put-call parity cannot be expressed as an equality but is expressed as a pair of inequalities:

$$[S - \mathrm{PV}(D)] - K \leq C(S, K, t, T) - P(S, K, t, T) \leq S - \mathrm{PV}(K).$$

- If the right-hand inequality is violated, $C - P \geq S - \mathrm{PV}(K)$, then we have the following arbitrage, if there is no early exercise:

Transaction	Initial (t) cashflow	Final (T) cashflow	
		$S(T) < 50$	$S(T) > 50$
Write a call	C	0	$-[S(T) - K]$
Buy a put	$-P$	$K - S(T)$	0
Buy a stock	$-S$	$S(T)$	$S(T)$
Borrow PV(K)	$\mathrm{PV}(K)$	$-K$	$-K$
	$(C - P) - (S - \mathrm{PV}(K))$	0	0

- Will there be early exercise? If yes, under what conditions?
- If the written call is exercised against you early at, say, time t', you sell the stock and repay the loan. Your net inflow is:

$$\left[-S(t') + K\right] + S(t') - Ke^{-r(T-t)} \times e^{r(t'-t)}$$
$$= K\left[1 - e^{-r(T-t')}\right] > 0$$

and you also retain the put.

- Going back to the table, why can't you borrow against the dividend? Because if you sell the stock before the dividend is paid you do not receive the dividend. *You cannot count on receiving the dividend.*

- If the left-hand inequality is violated, then $C-P \leq S-\text{PV}(D)-K$, and we have the following arbitrage:

Transaction	Initial (t) cashflow	Final (T) cashflow	
		$S(T) < K$	$S(T) > K$
Buy a call	$-C$	0	$S(T) - K$
Write a put	P	$-[K - S(T)]$	0
Short the stock	S	$-S(T)$	$-S(T)$
Lend K	$-K$	$Ke^{r(T-t)}$	$Ke^{r(T-t)}$
Lend PV(D)	$-\text{PV}(D)$		
	$[S-\text{PV}(D)-K] - [C - P] > 0$	>0	>0

- We have shown that the strategy is an arbitrage if your portfolio is held until maturity.
- What if the written put is exercised against you before maturity? Take your money out of the bank and close out your short position. Demonstrate that your net cash inflow is positive. In addition, you keep the live call as a bonus.
- Going back to the table, why do you have to lend K and not $\text{PV}(K)$? Because you need to count on having available K at any time that the put is exercised on you.

Summary

- Based on the assumption of no-arbitrage, we can prove a number of rules about option prices without making any assumptions about the behavior of the underlying security over time.
- To prove these rules, we show that if they fail, arbitrage opportunities will be present.
- Note that, in Chapter 2, we were able to derive exact pricing formulas for forwards and futures without making assumptions about the behavior of the underlying security over time. For stock options, however, we cannot derive exact pricing formulas *without* making assumptions about the dynamic behavior of stock prices. In this and the next lectures, we derive some general (inequality) pricing rules without assuming a dynamic model of stock price movement.
- Later on in the course, we introduce models for stock price dynamics and derive (equality) pricing formulas for stock options.

Assignment 3

1. (Review question) A one-year forward contract on a non-dividend-paying stock is entered into when the stock price is $50 and the risk-free interest rate is 5% per annum with continuous compounding.

   (a) What are the forward price and the initial value of the forward contract?
   (b) Six months after initiation of the forward contract, the price of the stock is $55 and the risk-free interest rate is still 5%. What is the new forward price for the same contract (which will now mature in 6 months)?
   (c) What is the value of the forward contract signed 6 months ago? Arrive at the answer by calculating the cashflows today associated with a set of actions that fully replicate the future cashflows associated with the forward position.

2. Suppose that you are the manager and sole owner of a highly leveraged firm. All the debt matures in one year. In one year, if the value of the firm is greater than the face value of the debt, you pay off the debt. If the value of the firm is less than the face value of the debt, you declare bankruptcy and the debt holders own the firm.

   (a) Express your position as an option on the value of the firm.
   (b) Express the position of the debt holders in terms of options on the value of the firm.
   (c) What can you do to increase the value of your position?

3. Intel is trading at $90 per share. An American call option on Intel with strike price $80 and 6 months to maturity is trading at $11. The risk-free interest rate is 8% (annualized continuous compounding). Intel will make a dividend payment in exactly one month and will not make any other dividend payment within the next 6 months. The amount of Intel dividend in one month is

not known yet and could lie anywhere between $1 per share and
$5 per share.

    (a) Do the above market prices provide an arbitrage opportunity?

    (b) If Intel announces that the dividend in one month will be
$1 per share and the above prices stay the same, would there
be an arbitrage opportunity?

4. A two-month European put option on a non-dividend-paying
stock is currently selling for $2. The stock price is $47, the strike
price is $50, and the risk-free interest rate is 6% (annualized,
continuous compounding).

    (a) What opportunities are there for an arbitrageur?

    (b) Would the above market price still provide an arbitrage
opportunity if the stock pays a dividend of $2/share in one
month?

5. Consider a forward contract with delivery price K and maturity
T on a stock that pays a continuous dividend yield of q.

    (a) Use the Put-Call Parity (for options on a stock with a
continuous dividend yield) to derive the formula for the value
of the forward contract.

    (b) Use the derived formula to calculate the market value of a
forward contract to purchase 1 million DM in 6 months at the
price of $0.65/DM. Assume that the US and German interest
rates are respectively, 5% and 7% (annualized continuous
compounding). The spot exchange rate is $0.66/DM.

6. Consider an American call with price C, an American put with
price P, both on the same stock with price S, common maturity
2 months, and common strike price K. The stock pays dividend
D and goes ex-dividend in one month from now.

    (a) Suppose that you observe that the put price is such that $P >
C - S + K + \text{PV}(D)$. Explain how you can beat the market.
Worry explicitly about the fact that the options are American

and that the options that you write may be exercised either rationally or irrationally.

(b) After you have established your above hedged position, suppose that the firm announces that it will postpone by three months the ex-dividend date. Assume that the announcement does not cause a change in the stock price. Do you become better off or worse off with this announcement? Explain.

7. Consider an at-the-money European call option and an at-the-money European put option. Which one has a higher theoretical market value?

8. *Note: For this problem you need to install Hull's "DERIVAGEM" software, which is on a CD on the back cover of the textbook.*

(a) Draw *by hand* graphs of European *and* American 3-month calls *and* puts, as functions of the (i) strike, (ii) maturity, (iii) volatility, and (iv) interest rate. The stock price is $50 and a $1 dividend is payable in one month from now. Set the volatility at 17%, the interest rate at 6%, and the strike at $50. As an aid in drawing these graphs, generate these graphs by using Hull's software that comes with the textbook.

(b) Print the graphs in (i) (but not in ii, iii, and iv) generated by Hull's software and attach them to your assignment.

Chapter 5

Trading Strategies and Slope and Convexity Restrictions

Agenda

- Introduction
- Graphs of European and American option prices as functions of the strike
- Slope restrictions
- Call and put spreads
- Convexity restrictions
- The butterfly spread
- The box spread

Introduction

In Chapter 4, we derived some basic no-arbitrage bounds on options prices and the put-call parity. In this chapter, we study some elementary trading strategies and, in the process, derive some no-arbitrage restrictions on the relationship between the prices of options that have different strike prices but are otherwise identical. Specifically, we place restrictions on how quickly the option price can change with the strike price (slope restrictions) and how quickly this slope changes with the strike price (convexity restrictions).

Example

We consider a 3-month derivative on a stock that has volatility 18% per year, current price $100, and pays a $5 dividend in one month from now. The c.c. rate of interest is 5% per year. In turn, we consider the derivative to be a European call, an American call, a European put, and an American put. We plot the price of the derivative as a function of its strike and provide the intuition for the main features of each graph.

European Call

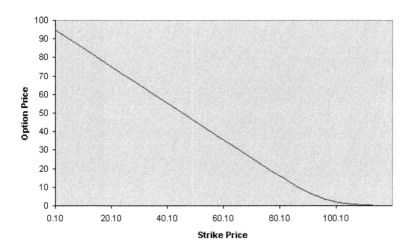

- At $K = 0$, $c = S_0 - \text{PV}(D) = 100 - \text{PV}(5) = 95.06$.
- The graph is downward-sloping.
- The slope starts at minus the present value factor, $-B(0,3$ months$)$, because potential exercise may occur in three months.
- The slope is flat when the strike is large.
- The graph is convex (the slope is increasing).
- The absolute value of the slope is between zero and $B(0,3$ months$)$.

American Call

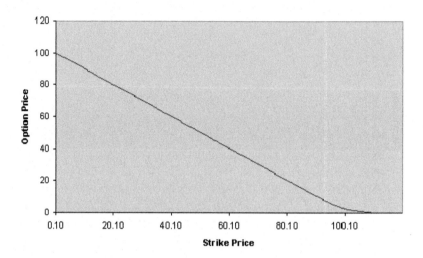

- At $K = 0$, the call price is $C = S_0 = 100$.
- The graph is downward-sloping.
- The slope starts at $-B(0, 1 \text{ month})$ because potential exercise may occur in 1 month.
- The slope is flat when the strike is large.
- The graph is convex (the slope is increasing).
- The absolute value of the slope is between zero and $B(0, 1 \text{ month})$.
- If there is no dividend, the slope starts at minus the present value factor, $B(0, 3 \text{ months})$, because potential exercise occurs only in three months.

European Put

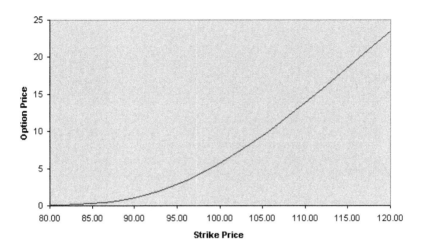

- At $K = 0$, the put price is zero.
- The graph is upward-sloping.
- The slope starts at zero.
- The slope tends to the present-value factor, $B(0, 3 \text{ months})$, as the strike increases.
- The graph is convex (the slope is increasing).
- The slope is between zero and $B(0, 3 \text{ months})$.

American Put

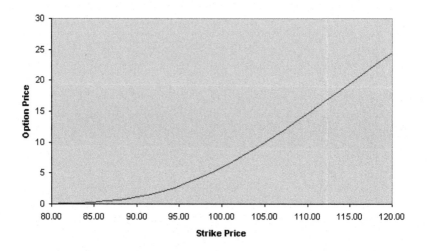

- At $K = 0$, the put price is zero.
- The graph is upward-sloping.
- The slope starts at zero.
- The slope tends to one as the strike increases.
- The graph is convex (the slope is increasing).
- The slope is between zero and one.

Slope Restrictions

- European call with or without dividends:

$$-B(0,T) \leq \frac{C(K_2) - C(K_1)}{K_2 - K_1} \leq 0.$$

- American call without dividends:

$$-B(0,T) \leq \frac{C(K_2) - C(K_1)}{K_2 - K_1} \leq 0.$$

- American call with dividend at t_D:

$$-B(0,t_D) \leq \frac{C(K_2) - C(K_1)}{K_2 - K_1} \leq 0.$$

- European put with or without dividends:

$$0 \leq \frac{P(K_2) - P(K_1)}{K_2 - K_1} \leq B(0,T).$$

- American put with or without dividends:

$$0 \leq \frac{P(K_2) - P(K_1)}{K_2 - K_1} \leq 1.$$

Example for European calls

IBM is currently trading at \$100. July 100 European calls are at \$8, and July 90 European calls are at \$19. Assume that the simple interest (not annualized) between now and the expiration date in July is 5%. The stock does pay dividend D in June.

- Since $(8 - 19)/(100 - 90) = -1.1 < -1/1.05$, there is an arbitrage opportunity that we exploit as follows:

Transaction	Payoff at t	Payoff at T		
		$S(T) < 90$	$90 \leq S(T) \leq 100$	$S(T) > 100$
Buy JUL 100	−\$8	0	0	$S(T) - 100$
Sell JUL 90	\$19	0	$-[S(T) - 90]$	$-[S(T) - 90]$
Lend	−\$9.52	10	10	10
	\$1.48	10	$0 \leq 100 - S(T) \leq 10$	0

- Note that dividends do not enter the arbitrage table because we are not trading the stock.
- A long call and a short call is a *call spread*. Call spreads are used in practice to make bets on the direction of the future stock price.
- In the call spread in the table, we make a bet that the stock price will *fall*. This is an example of a *bear spread*.
- Draw the payoff of a long position in the JUL 100 call.
- Draw the payoff of a short position in the JUL 90 call.
- Draw the net payoff of a long position in the JUL 100 call and the short position in the JUL 90 call. This is the payoff of a call spread, betting that the stock price will *fall*.
- To the above net payoff, add $10 to replicate the payoff in the arbitrage table.

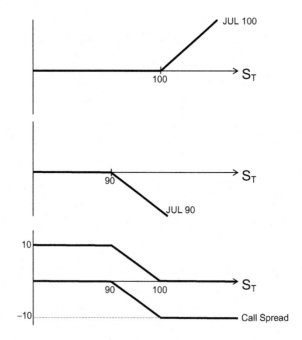

- As another example, if we buy the JUL 90 call and sell the JUL 100 call, we bet that the stock price will *increase*. Whereas we could make such a bet by simply buying the JUL 90 call, by selling the JUL 100 call, we partly finance the purchase of the JUL 90 call. This is an example of a *bull spread*.

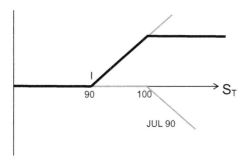

Example for American Calls

Suppose the calls are American. Since $(8 - 19)/(100 - 90) = -1.1 < -1$ there is still an arbitrage opportunity.

- We exploit it by modifying the above table as follows: lend $10 instead of PV(10).
- If we are assigned, we close out all positions and still come ahead. Closing out all positions is an easy response for the purpose of demonstrating that we come out ahead. It is not the best response.

Example for European Puts

IBM is currently trading at $100. July 100 puts are at 2\frac{1}{2}$, and July 110 puts are at 12\frac{1}{4}$. Your cost of money (simple rate) is 5% between now and the option maturity.

- Since $(12.25 - 2.5)/(110 - 100) = 0.975 > 1/1.05$, there is an arbitrage opportunity that we exploit as follows:

Transaction	Payoff at t	$S(T) < 100$	$100 \leq S(T) \leq 110$	$S(T) > 110$
			Payoff at T	
Buy JUL 100	−$2.5	$100 - S(T)$	0	0
Sell JUL 110	$12.25	$-[110 - S(T)]$	$-[110 - S(T)]$	0
Lend	−$9.52	10	10	10
$0.226	0	$S(T) - 100 > 0$	10	

- Note that dividends do not enter the arbitrage table because we are not trading the stock.
- A long put and a short put is a *put spread*. Put spreads are used in practice to make bets on the direction of the future stock price.
- In the put spread in the table, we make a bet that the stock price will *increase*. This is a *bull spread*.

Suppose the puts are American. Since $(12.25 - 2.5)/(110 - 100) = 0.975 < 1$, there is no arbitrage opportunity.

- Draw the payoff of a long position in the JUL 100 put.
- Draw the payoff of a short position in the JUL 110 put.
- Draw the net payoff of a long position in the JUL 100 put and the short position in the JUL 110 put. This is the payoff of a *put spread*, betting that the stock price will *increase*.
- To the above net payoff, add \$10 to replicate the payoff in the arbitrage table.

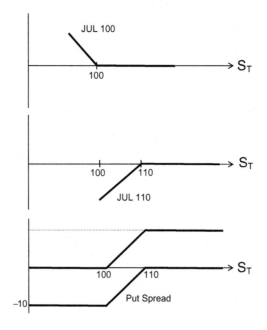

Convexity Restrictions

- Consider three strikes, K_1, K_2, K_3, such that $K_1 \leq K_2 \leq K_3$.
- For European and American calls with or without dividends, the slope of the call price as a function of the strike is increasing in the strike price:

$$\frac{C(K_3) - C(K_2)}{K_3 - K_2} \geq \frac{C(K_2) - C(K_1)}{K_2 - K_1}.$$

- For European and American puts with or without dividends, the slope of the put price as a function of the strike is increasing in the strike price:

$$\frac{P(K_3) - P(K_2)}{K_3 - K_2} \geq \frac{P(K_2) - P(K_1)}{K_2 - K_1}.$$

Example for American puts

IBM is currently trading at $\$48\frac{1}{8}$. June 65 puts are at 17, June 70 puts are at 22, and June 75 puts are at 26. Your cost of money is 3.25%/year. What is the arbitrage opportunity and how can it be exploited?

			Payoff at T		
Transaction	Payoff at t	$S(T) < 65$	$65 \leq S(T)$ < 70	$70 \leq S(T)$ ≤ 75	$S(T) > 75$
Buy JUN 65	$-\$17$	$65 - S(T)$	0	0	0
Sell 2 JUN 70	$\$44$	$-2[70 - S(T)]$	$-2[70 - S(T)]$	0	0
Buy JUN 75	$-\$26$	$75 - S(T)$	$75 - S(T)$	$75 - S(T)$	0
	$\$1$	0	$S(T) - 65$	$75 - S(T)$	0

- If we are *assigned* on the June 70 puts, we close out all positions and still come ahead. Closing out all positions is an easy response for the purpose of demonstrating that we come out ahead. It is not the best response.

- The position taken in the table with puts with three different strikes is called a *put butterfly spread*. The corresponding position but with calls is called a *call butterfly spread*.
- Note that dividends do not enter the arbitrage table because we are not trading the stock.
- A butterfly spread is a *trade in volatility*. We are *selling volatility*: We are betting that the volatility will be lower than what the market thinks it will be.
- Think of the trades in the table as (1) a put spread consisting of buying one JUN 65 put and writing one JUN 70 put; and (2) a put spread consisting of buying the JUN 75 put and writing one JUN 70 put.
- Draw the payoff of the put spread consisting of buying one JUN 65 put and writing one JUN 70 put.
- Draw the payoff of the put spread consisting of buying one JUN 75 put and writing one JUN 70 put.
- Draw the net payoff of positions (1) and (2).

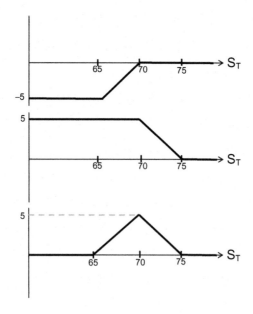

European Box Spread

- For European calls and puts with common expiration, no-arbitrage requires the following:

$$\underbrace{\frac{[c(K_1) - p(K_1)]}{\substack{synthetic\ long \\ forward, delivery \\ price\ K_1}}} - \underbrace{\frac{[c(K_2) - p(K_2)]}{\substack{synthetic\ short \\ forward, delivery \\ price\ K_2}}} = PV(K_2 - K_1).$$

- We can prove it by subtracting the put-call parity for strike K_2 from the put-call parity for strike K_1.
- The relation holds with or without dividends.
- An attractive feature of the box spread is that all trades take place on one exchange and it does not involve the more cumbersome trading in the stock.
- For American calls and puts, the corresponding expression is

$$PV(K_2 - K_1) \leq [C(K_1) - P(K_1)] - [C(K_2) - P(K_2)]$$

and

$$[C(K_1) - P(K_1)] - [C(K_2) - P(K_2)] \leq K_2 - PV(K_1) + PV(D).$$

We do not study it because it is not useful in practice.

Example of European Box Spread Violation

- Assume that $K_1 = 45$, $K_2 = 55$ and

$$[c(45) - p(45)] - [c(55) - p(55)] < PV(10).$$

- Then there is the following arbitrage opportunity:

ACTION	INFLOW	$S_T < 45$	$45 \leq S_T < 55$	$55 \leq S_T$
Buy c(45)	$-c(45)$	0	$S_T - 45$	$S_T - 45$
Write p(45)	$p(45)$	$-(45 - S_T)$	0	0
Write c(55)	$c(55)$	0	0	$-(S_T - 55)$
Buy p(55)	$-p(55)$	$55 - S_T$	$55 - S_T$	0
Borrow PV(10)	$PV(10)$	-10	-10	-10
NET	>0	0	0	0

- An interesting interpretation of the actions taken is: (1) a long forward position with delivery price 45 and (2) a short forward position with delivery price 55.

Chapter 6

Optimal Early Exercise
of American Options

Agenda

- Introduction and motivation
- Intuition behind early exercise
- Example on the exercise of an American call when the stock does not pay dividend
- Summary of the rules
- The dividend spread

Introduction and Motivation

- Using only basic arbitrage arguments, we develop the most specific rules we can about when it is optimal to exercise options prior to maturity.
- Even though later on we develop exact early exercise rules using exact option pricing, the rules developed here are important because they do not require the additional assumptions required for exact option pricing. These rules hold no matter what process is assumed for the stock price.

Intuition Behind Early Exercise

- For a call on stock that does not pay dividends:

$$C \geq c = S - \text{PV}(K) + p$$

$$= \underbrace{S - K}_{\substack{\text{proceeds of} \\ \text{early exercise}}} + \underbrace{K - \text{PV}(K)}_{\substack{\text{interest lost} \\ \text{in early exercise}}} + \underbrace{p}_{\substack{\text{downside} \\ \text{risk protection}}}.$$

The live call is more valuable than the proceeds of early exercise.

- For a put on stock that does not pay dividends:

$$P \geq p = c - S + \text{PV}(K)$$

$$= \underbrace{K - S}_{\substack{\text{proceeds of} \\ \text{early exercise}}} - \underbrace{K - \text{PV}(K)}_{\substack{\text{interest gained} \\ \text{in early exercise}}} + \underbrace{c}_{\substack{\text{upside gain} \\ \text{potential}}}.$$

Ambiguous case. The proceeds of early exercise are more valuable than the live put, if the put is deep in the money.

- For a call on stock that pays dividends:

$$C \geq c = S - \text{PV}(K) + p - \text{PV}(D)$$

$$= \underbrace{S - K}_{\substack{\text{proceeds of} \\ \text{early exercise}}} + \underbrace{K - \text{PV}(K)}_{\substack{\text{interest lost in} \\ \text{early exercise}}} + \underbrace{p}_{\substack{\text{downside} \\ \text{risk protection}}} - \text{PV}(D).$$

Ambiguous case. The live call is more valuable than the proceeds of early exercise, unless the call is deep in the money and the record date on a dividend is imminent.

- For a put on stock that pays dividends:

$$P \geq p = c - S + \text{PV}(K) + \text{PV}(D)$$

$$= \underbrace{K - S}_{\substack{\text{proceeds of} \\ \text{early exercise}}} - \underbrace{K - \text{PV}(K)}_{\substack{\text{interest gained} \\ \text{in early exercise}}} + \underbrace{c}_{\substack{\text{upside gain} \\ \text{potential}}} + \text{PV}(D).$$

Ambiguous case. The live put is more valuable than the proceeds of early exercise, unless it is deep in the money. The dividend makes early exercise less attractive.

Example on the Exercise of an American Call when the Stock Does Not Pay Dividend

- Consider an American call on Intel with $K = 100$ and $T - t = 3$ months, and currently $S = 105$. The *simple* interest rate between now and the option maturity is $R(t, T) = 1\%$. Should you exercise now, or wait until maturity?
- We know that

$$C \geq c = S - \text{PV}(K) + p = [S - K] + [K - \text{PV}(K)] + p.$$

If we exercise the option, we get $105 - 100 = 5$. By selling now, we get *at least* $105 - \text{PV}(100) = 6$, about \$1.00 more than by exercising. We should wait until maturity.

What if you cannot sell the option?

- **Strategy A**: Exercise now. Pay $K = 100$ today. Get one share of stock, which in 3 months will be worth $S(T)$.
- **Strategy B**: Delay exercise until maturity. Instead of exercising, take the $K = 100$ and buy a bond, which will be worth 101 in 3 months. At maturity, we have two scenarios:

  - If $S(T) > 100$, exercise the option, paying 100 for the stock. You end up with one share plus \$101 − \$100 = \$1 in cash.
  - If $S(T) \leq 100$, say $S(T) = 98$, do not exercise the option. Buy one share for 98. You end up with one share plus \$101−\$98 = \$3 in cash.

What if you know the stock price is going to fall?
You are tempted to exercise now and take your profits (sell the stock) rather than wait and have the option expire worthless. What is the solution to this paradox?

- If you think that the stock is going to fall, short the stock rather than exercising now. We can show that we can assure ourselves of a higher payoff with this strategy. Compare the two strategies.

- **Strategy A'**: Exercise now paying $K = 100$ to get 1 share of stock. Sell the stock to get $S(t) = 105$. Invest $\$105 - \$100 = \$5$ for 3 months until time T to get $\$5.01$.
- **Strategy B'**: Delay exercise until maturity. Today short stock to get $S(t) = 105$. Invest 105 in the risk-free asset for 3 months until time T, when proceeds will be worth 106.05. After 3 months (at time T) we have two scenarios:

$$\text{if } \begin{cases} S(T) > 100, & \text{exercise option, paying } K \text{ for stock} \\ S(T) < 100, & \text{do not exercise, buy stock for } S(T). \end{cases}$$

Use the stock to cover the short position. The payoff in 3 months (at T) is $106.05 - \min[100, S(T)]$ which is *a minimum* of $\$6.05$, and more if $S(T) < 100$.

- Just as before, the intuition is that if you exercise early you lose both (1) the time value of money on the $100 exercise price and (2) the value of the right not to exercise.
- If the stock pays dividend, it is sometimes worthwhile to exercise the call just before the payment of a large dividend.
- The stock price will drop by the amount of the dividend on the ex-date. If the value of the dividend is greater than the interest you lose on the exercise price plus the option value, then it is worthwhile to exercise.

Summary of Rules for American Calls

- Never exercise early an American call on a stock that does not pay dividends over the life of the option.
- If an American call is ITM at maturity, then exercise it.
- The only times to consider early exercise of an American call are the times *just* before the dividend record dates.

Summary of Rules for American Puts

- It is never optimal to exercise an American put just before a dividend record date.
- At all other dates, it may or may not be optimal to exercise the put at time t. Before we can figure this out, we need to develop the binomial option pricing model.

The Dividend Spread

An Example

- Suppose that the stock price today is $50. Tomorrow a $1 dividend is payable on the stock. That is, today is the *dividend record date*. To keep our example simple, we assume that no more dividends are payable over the next month.
- As is almost always the case, the stock price drops by the full amount of the dividend and, therefore, the after-dividend stock price is $49.
- We assume that the annualized stock volatility is 20% and the annualized, c.c. interest rate over the next month is 10%.
- As a preliminary calculation, let us find the price of a one-month call with strike 40.

  — If we exercise the call today, we receive $50 − $40 = $10.
  — If we leave the call unexercised, we miss the dividend and end up holding a call on stock that has price $49. By the Black–Scholes–Merton (BSM) formula, the call price tomorrow is $9.33.
  — Thus it is optimal to exercise the call today. If we don't, we throw away $10 − $9.33 = $0.67.
  — However, as Emperor Nero said, *pecunia non olet.*

Institutional Background

- You can exercise any long calls in your opening position. Obviously if you are long 100 calls and you hold them all day you can exercise them. What is less intuitive is that if you are long 100 calls to begin the day and you sell them out during the day, you can still exercise 100 calls. Furthermore, if you are long 100 and you sell 200 you can still exercise 100. These exercises are referred to as "on sheets" exercises, meaning the positions are on your morning bank/clearing firm statements.

- The second part regards what are called "same-day" exercises, the obvious implication is that the transactions took place on the same day you are planning to exercise them. These are governed by the simple, but strange, rule that you can exercise any positive transactions. So if I buy 10 options and sell 30 of the same options on the same day, I can still exercise 10 options.

Strategy

- One day before the stock goes ex-dividend, Jack buys 1000 call contracts (100,000 calls) from Jill. Also, Jill buys 1000 call contracts from Jack at the same price. This is a wash for both Jack and Jill.
- The exchange agrees to cap the transaction fees because they just want to be able to show investors that their exchange has the most volume.
- On the same day, Jill exercises her long calls, receives 100,000 shares, and pays $4 million. She hopes that she is not assigned on her short calls.
- If Jill is assigned, she delivers the shares in her short position and receives $4 million. For Jill, this is a wash. She only loses her initial transaction fee.
- If Jill is not assigned, she receives $100,000 dividend, sells the stock for $4.9 million, and buys 1000 call contracts for $933,000. Her long calls effectively close out her short position in calls.
- The net profit for Jill is $100,000 + $4,900,000 − $4,000,000 − $933,000 = $67,000.
- Jack, who always follows Jill's example, makes $67,000 too if he is not assigned!

Assignment 4

1. Indicate whether the following statements are true or false or neither, and explain your answer. For questions (a) and (b), the following data applies. The current stock price is $100 and the present value of $1 payable in 6 months is $0.95. There are no dividend record dates over the next six months and all options on this stock are American.

   (a) The market price of a call option expiring in 6 months with a strike price of $90 must lie between $10 and $14.50 to avoid arbitrage.

   (b) If the market price of a put option expiring in 6 months with a strike price of $105 is $5.50 then the price of an otherwise similar call on the stock should not be less than $0.50 to avoid arbitrage.

   (c) A rational American put holder would only consider early exercise immediately after a dividend or at maturity.

   (d) If the interest rate, dividend, and stock price do not change, an increase in stock volatility and skewness that increases the price of a European call by $0.50 will increase the price of a European put on the same stock, same exercise price, and same maturity by $0.50 also.

2. What is your bet if you are holding a butterfly spread? What is your bet if you are holding a bottom straddle?

3. You are given the following two sets of prices of European options as a function of the strike price, for a stock with $S = 100$. Assume that all options mature in 6 months and that the interest rate (annualized, c.c.) is 10%.

   (1) $p(90) = 4$, $\quad p(100) = 9\frac{1}{8}$, $\quad p(110) = 16$, $\quad p(120) = 25\frac{3}{4}$.
   (2) $p(90) = 2\frac{3}{4}$, $\quad p(100) = 8\frac{1}{2}$, $\quad p(110) = 17$, $\quad p(120) = 24$.

   For each set of prices, please answer the following questions.

   (a) Assume that the stock will not pay any dividend in the next 6 months. Do these prices satisfy no-arbitrage restrictions on option values? If yes, prove it. If not, construct an arbitrage portfolio to realize riskless profits and show how that portfolio performs under different market conditions. (You may use an arbitrage table.)

(b) Does your answer to part (a) change if these put options are American? Explain.

(c) Does your answer to part (a) change if the stock pays an unknown amount of dividend in 3 months? Explain.

4. Given the following prices of American options as a function of the strike price, for a stock with $S = 50$, find the arbitrage opportunities in each of the price sets below if they exist. If there is more than one arbitrage opportunity, just discuss one of them. Use a table to prove that your position is an arbitrage position. Assume that all options mature in 6 months, that the six-month *simple* interest rate is 5%, and that there are no dividends paid on the stock. *Be sure to state how you deal with early exercise.*

(a) $P(40) = 32$, $P(45) = 35\frac{1}{2}$, $P(50) = 39\frac{1}{4}$, $P(55) = 44$.

(b) $C(45) = 8$, $C(50) = 4$, $P(45) = 1$, $P(50) = 4.50$.

(c) $P(60) = 14$, $P(65) = 16\frac{1}{2}$, $P(70) = 19\frac{3}{4}$, $P(75) = 24$.

5. IBM is trading at $52. IBM will pay a dividend in 2 months. This is the only dividend that will be paid over the next three months. The annualized c.c. interest rate is 6%.

(a) You hold an American put option on IBM with an exercise price of 40 that matures in 3 months. Suppose that the dividend in 2 months is at least $0.50. Should you exercise the put at any time before the ex-dividend date? Why?

(b) You hold an American call option on IBM with an exercise price of 50 that matures in 3 months.

- Should you exercise your call option in 1 month if the stock price has gone up a lot by then?
- Suppose that the dividend in 2 months is at most $0.20. Should you exercise your call option just before the dividend?

- Suppose that the dividend in 2 months will be $0.40. Do you have enough information to know for sure whether you want to exercise your call option just before the dividend?

6. Do the following prices of American options (as a function of the strike price), for a stock with S = 50, provide an arbitrage opportunity? If yes, what is your arbitrage strategy and payoff? Assume that all options mature in 6 months, and that the six-month *simple* interest rate is 5% and that there are no dividends paid on the stock. *Be sure to state how you deal with early exercise.*

$$C(40) = 20, \quad C(45) = 17, \quad C(55) = 10.$$

(The $C(50)$ call is not traded)

7. A stock is trading at $50 per share and the company will pay a dividend of $3 per share in 4 months but no more dividends within one year. An American call option with a strike price of $40 and 6 months to maturity is trading at $11. Assume that the interest rate (annualized, c.c.) is 12%. Prove that the option price satisfies all of the no-arbitrage bound restrictions that we have derived. However, you still *can* find an arbitrage opportunity. What is your arbitrage strategy?

Chapter 7

Binomial Option Pricing

When you come to a fork in the road, take it — Yogi Berra

Agenda

- Introduction
- Example of one-stage binomial pricing
- The general one-stage binomial model
- Risk-adjusted probabilities
- The Black–Scholes–Merton insight
- Example of two-stage binomial pricing
- The general binomial model
- Dynamic replication
- Portfolio insurance
- Leland–O'Brien–Rubinstein (LOR)

Introduction

- We show that, if stock prices move in a particular way, we can create a *synthetic call* by applying a *dynamic trading strategy*.
- We show later on that this assumption about stock price movements is plausible, but only under certain circumstances.
- The *replicating portfolio* consists of a continually changing leveraged stock position.
- The payoff of the replicating portfolio is equal to the payoff of the call that we are replicating.
- Therefore, *the call price is equal the price of the replicating portfolio of stock and bonds.* If it is not, an arbitrage opportunity exists.
- Black and Scholes (1973) use this same insight to derive their famous option pricing formula. Their approach involves the mathematics of "stochastic calculus".
- The mathematics of the binomial approach is simple, and, *in the limit,* is identical to that of Black and Scholes.

Example of one-stage binomial pricing

- Assume that the current interest rate over the "period" is 20%, the current stock price is 60 and the stock price can either fall to 30 or rise to 90 at the end of the period.

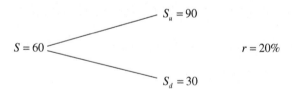

- At the end of the period, a call with strike price 60 will be worth either 30 or 0.

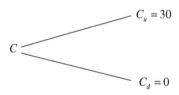

- Suppose we buy one-half share and borrow $12.50.

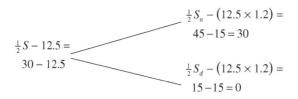

$$\tfrac{1}{2}S - 12.5 =$$
$$30 - 12.5$$

$$\tfrac{1}{2}S_u - \left(12.5 \times 1.2\right) =$$
$$45 - 15 = 30$$

$$\tfrac{1}{2}S_d - \left(12.5 \times 1.2\right) =$$
$$15 - 15 = 0$$

- Since this portfolio represents the payoff to the call, the call must have the same value as the portfolio:

$$C = \frac{S}{2} - 12.50 = 30 - 12.50 = 17.50.$$

- Therefore, this call is worth 17.50.

What if the call option is trading at $18.50?

- We then have an arbitrage opportunity, since we can replicate the payoff of the call option by spending only $17.50.
- To explore the arbitrage opportunity, we form the following portfolio:

  ➤ Write one call option;
  ➤ Buy the replicating portfolio of stocks and bonds for the call option; that is, buy one half share of the stock and borrow $12.50.

- The cash inflow at time 0 is $1.00.
- The payoff from the replicating portfolio, by design, exactly covers the written-option obligation.

What if the call option is trading at $16.50?

Reverse the above positions and still realize a $1.00 arbitrage profit.

Important observation: The option price does not explicitly depend on the probabilities.

- Our calculation is based on a no-arbitrage argument. Since an arbitrage strategy gives a positive payoff regardless of whether the stock goes up or down, an arbitrage-based argument does not depend on the probabilities of the two scenarios.

- Given that the stock's future returns are already reflected in its current price S_t, we no longer need to consider the stock's future returns when we derive the relationship between the call price and the stock price.

- A news event that leads to an increase in the assessed probability for an up-move in the stock price does affect the value of the call option indirectly by affecting the stock price.

How Did We Guess the Replicating Portfolio?

- We need to solve for the replicating portfolio by using the conditions that the portfolio generates the same payoffs as the option in both states.

- Suppose a portfolio of Δ shares of stocks and a loan L replicates the call payoff.

If the stock price increases to $90, the payoff is:

$$90\Delta - 1.2L = 30. \tag{1}$$

If the stock price decreases to 30, the payoff is:

$$30\Delta - 1.2L = 0. \tag{2}$$

- Solving Eqs. (1) and (2) we find

$$\Delta = \frac{30 - 0}{90 - 30} = \frac{1}{2} \quad \text{and} \quad L = 12.5.$$

- We call Δ the *hedge ratio* of the call.

- Thus, *a synthetic call is a levered position in a fraction of one share.*

The General One-Stage Binomial Model

Let:

$u = 1+$ rate of return if the stock goes up;
$d = 1+$ rate of return if the stock goes down;
$\bar{r} = 1+$ interest rate for borrowing and lending.

- No arbitrage between the stock and the borrowing/lending opportunity imposes the following restriction between the parameters u, d, and $\bar{r}$:

$$d < \bar{r} < u.$$

- If $\bar{r} < d < u$, we make an arbitrage profit by borrowing and buying the stock.
- If $d < u < \bar{r}$, we make an arbitrage profit by shorting the stock and lending.

The stock payoff is then:

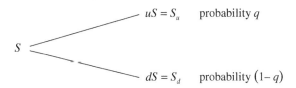

and the call option's payoff (at maturity) is:

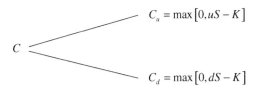

We can create a portfolio where we buy Δ shares and borrow $\$L$ at the risk-free rate.

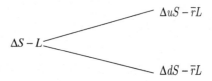

$$\Delta S - L \begin{cases} \Delta u S - \bar{r}L \\ \\ \Delta d S - \bar{r}L \end{cases}$$

- We want to replicate the call, so we require that:

$$\Delta u S - \bar{r}L = C_u, \tag{3}$$

$$\Delta d S - \bar{r}L = C_d. \tag{4}$$

- Computing the hedge ratio Δ yields:

$$\Delta = \frac{C_u - C_d}{uS - dS} > 0.$$

- Computing the face value of the debt using Eqs. (3) and (4) yields:

$$L = \frac{dC_u - uC_d}{\bar{r}(u - d)}.$$

- Note that L is always positive for a call:

  Part of the stock purchase in the replicating portfolio for a call is financed by borrowing.

- If we wish to replicate the payoffs of a put, we solve the following pair of equations:

$$\Delta u S - \bar{r}\, L = \max[0, K - uS]$$

and

$$\Delta d S - \bar{r}\, L = \max[0, K - dS].$$

Risk-Adjusted Probabilities

- Our pricing of the call or put in the previous example has the following interpretation which is very powerful and useful in the industry in pricing derivatives.
- We calculated the hedge ratio of a call as $\Delta = \frac{C_u - C_d}{uS - dS}$, and the borrowed amount as $L = \frac{dC_u - uC_d}{\bar{r}(u-d)}$.
- By no-arbitrage, the price of a call should be:

$$
\begin{aligned}
C &= \Delta S - L \\
&= \frac{C_u - C_d}{u - d} - \frac{dC_u - uC_d}{\bar{r}(u - d)}.
\end{aligned}
$$

Rearrange as:

$$
\begin{aligned}
C &= \frac{1}{\bar{r}} \left(\frac{\bar{r} - d}{u - d} \right) C_u + \frac{1}{\bar{r}} \left(\frac{u - \bar{r}}{u - d} \right) C_d \\
&= \frac{pC_u + (1 - p)C_d}{\bar{r}},
\end{aligned}
$$

where we define

$$
p = \frac{\bar{r} - d}{u - d} \quad \text{and} \quad 1 - p = 1 - \frac{\bar{r} - d}{u - d} = \frac{u - \bar{r}}{u - d}.
$$

- The no-arbitrage condition $d < \bar{r} < u$ guarantees that p is positive and $1 - p$ is positive. Therefore, p is a number between zero and one and qualifies to be thought of as a "probability".
- Then the equation $C = \frac{pC_u + (1-p)C_d}{\bar{r}}$ has the following interpretation. If we think of p as the "probability" that the stock price goes up, the numerator is the "expected price of the call". This expected price is discounted at the risk-free rate of interest.
- Since we do not account for risk with a risk premium on the discount rate, it must be that the "probability p" adjusts for risk.

- Thus, we interpret p as the *risk-adjusted probability* that the stock price goes up. This probability is sometimes referred to as the "risk-neutral" probability even though the term "risk neutral" is misleading.
- The risk-adjusted probability is typically different from the real probability. Do not confuse the two.
- The result that we just derived is very general and, as we shall see later, very useful in practice. The general result states:

> *"Absence of arbitrage implies the existence of risk-adjusted probabilities such that any derivative is priced as its expected payoff using the risk-adjusted probabilities and discounted at the risk free rate of interest"*

- In our example, absence of arbitrage requires that $d < \bar{r} < u$, which in turn implies that $p = \frac{\bar{r}-d}{u-d} > 0$ *and* $1 - p = \frac{u-\bar{r}}{u-d} > 0$. Therefore, p and $1-p$ are interpreted as risk-adjusted probabilities.
- We could have found p directly by arguing as follows. The stock has payoffs uS and dS. The expected payoff on the stock, using the risk-adjusted probabilities is $puS + (1 - p)dS$. Discounting the expected payoff at the risk-free rate should give us today's stock price:

$$\frac{puS + (1 - p)dS}{\bar{r}} = S.$$

We solve for p and obtain $p = \frac{\bar{r}-d}{u-d}$.

The Black–Scholes–Merton Insight

- Black, Scholes and Merton (BSM) worked within the mathematically challenging framework of "stochastic calculus". In this course, we do not use stochastic calculus. However, we can explain the BSM intuition in the context of binomial trees.
- Obviously, stock prices can take on more than two values. Thus we wish to extend the binomial tree to one with many branches.
- The replication in the above example does not work if the tree is "trinomial", that is, if it has three branches. Why? Because we have three equations to satisfy but only two variables, Δ and L.
- The major insight here is that "under certain circumstances" *we can increase the number of possible outcomes of the stock price by shortening the time period of each step and taking more steps.*
- Start thinking about what these circumstances are. The key concept here is *liquidity*. Later on, we will talk about two cases where lack of liquidity was the reason for their demise: Leland–O'Brien–Rubinstein (LOR) and long-term capital management (LTCM).

Example of two-stage binomial pricing

- ABC's stock is trading at $10 per share. The stock price will either go up or go down by 20% for each of the next two years. The risk-free annual simple interest rate is 10%. What is the price of a 2-year call option on the stock with a strike price of $8?
- The binomial-tree model parameters for the stock price are: $u = 1.2$, $d = 0.8$, $\bar{r} = 1.1$. Therefore, $p = \frac{\bar{r}-d}{u-d} = 0.75$.

- The stock-price and option-price binomial trees are:

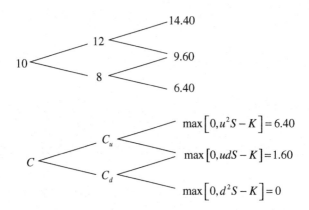

- The call prices in 1 year are:

- $C_u = \dfrac{pC_{uu} + (1-p)C_{ud}}{\bar{r}} = \dfrac{0.75 \times 6.4 + 0.25 \times 1.6}{1.1} = 4.73$

and

- $C_d = \dfrac{pC_{ud} + (1-p)C_{dd}}{\bar{r}} = \dfrac{0.75 \times 1.6 + 0.25 \times 0}{1.1} = 1.09.$

- Today's call price is:

$$C = \frac{pC_u + (1-p)C_d}{\bar{r}} = \frac{0.75 \times 4.73 + 0.25 \times 1.09}{1.1} = 3.47.$$

- We repeat the above example with symbols in order to illustrate the power of working with risk-adjusted probabilities.
- The stock-price and option-price binomial trees are:

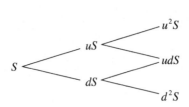

and

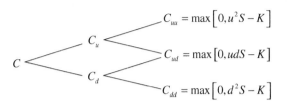

- The call prices in one year are:

$$C_u = \frac{pC_{uu} + (1-p)C_{ud}}{\bar{r}},$$

$$C_d = \frac{pC_{ud} + (1-p)C_{dd}}{\bar{r}}.$$

- Today's call price is:

$$C = \frac{pC_u + (1-p)C_d}{\bar{r}},$$

$$C = \frac{p^2 C_{uu} + p(1-p)C_{ud} + (1-p)pC_{du} + (1-p)^2 C_{dd}}{\bar{r}^2}$$

$$= \frac{p^2 C_{uu} + 2p(1-p)C_{ud} + (1-p)^2 C_{dd}}{\bar{r}^2}.$$

- Again, this is the "expectation" of the discounted future value using the risk-adjusted probabilities:

$$\text{Prob}[C_{uu}] = p^2,$$

$$\text{Prob}[C_{ud}] = 2p(1-p),$$

$$\text{Prob}[C_{dd}] = (1-p)^2.$$

Dynamic Replication

- Although it is easy to price derivatives by using the risk-adjusted probabilities, this method can obscure what is really behind our pricing approach.
- The risk-adjusted pricing method gives the correct option price because it gives the cost of replicating the option's payoff.
- We illustrated how to replicate a call option in a one-period binomial model.
- Here we illustrate how we can *dynamically* replicate an option's payoffs in a two-period binomial-tree model.
- We again use the previous two-period example:

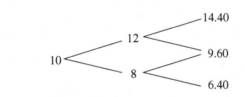

$u = 1.2$, $d = 0.8$, $\bar{r} = 1.1$, $p = 0.75$.
- From our previous risk-adjusted calculation,

$$C = 3.47, \quad C_u = 4.73, \quad C_d = 1.09.$$

- **At time 0:** The replicating portfolio at time 0, with Δ shares and L in borrowing, should have value 4.73 if the stock goes up and 1.09 if the stock goes down:

$$\Delta = \frac{C_u - C_d}{uS - dS} = \frac{4.73 - 1.09}{12 - 8} = 0.91.$$

We can find the borrowed amount by either using the formula,

$$L = \frac{dC_u - uC_d}{\bar{r}(u - d)} = 5.63$$

or reason as follows: the total cost of purchasing 0.91 shares is $9.10. Since the out-of-pocket cost should be $3.47, the borrowed amount is $9.10 - 3.47 = 5.63$.

- **At node u at time 1**: The replicating portfolio for the call option has Δ_u shares and L_u in borrowing:

$$\Delta_u = \frac{C_{uu} - C_{ud}}{uuS - udS} = \frac{6.4 - 1.6}{14.4 - 9.6} = 1.0,$$

$$L_u = \frac{dC_{uu} - uC_{ud}}{\bar{r}(u - d)} = \frac{0.8 \times 6.40 - 1.2 \times 1.60}{1.1 \times (1.2 - 0.8)} = 7.27.$$

- Check that 1.0 share plus 7.27 in borrowing indeed replicates the option's payoff at time 2:
At node uu: $1.0 \cdot uuS - \bar{r} \cdot 7.27 = 6.40$,
At node ud: $1.0 \cdot udS - \bar{r} \cdot 7.27 = 1.60$.
The cost of the node-u replicating portfolio at u is

$$\Delta_u \cdot uS - L_u = 1.0 \cdot 12 - 7.27 = 4.73,$$

which is exactly the node-u option price C_u that we calculated with the risk-adjustment method.
- **At node d at time 1**: The replicating portfolio for the call option has Δ_d shares and L_d in borrowing:

$$\Delta_d = \frac{C_{ud} - C_{dd}}{udS - ddS} = \frac{1.6 - 0}{9.6 - 6.4} = 0.5,$$

$$L_d = \frac{dC_{ud} - uC_{dd}}{\bar{r}(u - d)} = 2.91.$$

Check that 0.5 shares plus 2.91 in borrowing indeed replicates the option's payoff at time 2:
At node ud: $0.5 \cdot udS - \bar{r} \cdot 2.91 = 1.6$,
At node dd: $0.5 \cdot udS - \bar{r} \cdot 2.91 = 0$.

The cost of the node-d replicating portfolio at d is

$$\Delta_d \cdot dS - L_d = 0.5 \cdot 8 - 2.91 = 1.09$$

which is exactly the node-d option price C_d that we calculated by the risk-adjusted method.
At node u: $0.91 \cdot uS - \bar{r} \cdot 5.63 = 4.73$,
At node d: $0.91 \cdot dS - \bar{r} \cdot 5.63 = 1.09$.
The cost of the replicating portfolio at time 0 is:

$$\Delta \cdot S - L = 0.91 \cdot 10 - 5.63 = 3.47,$$

which is exactly the option price C that we calculated by the risk-adjusted method.

- Why is the value of the call $3.47? It is the cost of a portfolio that provides us with payoffs of $4.73 if the stock goes up and $1.09 if the stock goes down. With $4.73 at node u and $1.09 at node d, we can purchase the replicating portfolios at u and d. The u and d replicating portfolio have the same time-2 final payoffs as those of the option.

- Why call it *dynamic replication?* We cannot replicate the time-2 option payoffs by buying a portfolio of stocks and bonds and holding it until time 2. That is, we cannot have a *static replication.* To replicate the time-2 option payoffs, we have to change the composition of our replicating portfolio at every time period.

- How do we arbitrage if the option is mispriced? Suppose that the option price is $3.70 at time 0.

- To arbitrage, we write the (expensive) call option at $3.70 and buy the (cheap) replicating portfolio at $3.47, and pocket the difference of $0.23.

- At time 1, we change the composition of the replicating portfolio.

- Repeat the example on pages 19–23 to make a synthetic long position in a European *put* option. Show that the hedge ratio is negative, therefore we short the stock. As the stock price falls, we short an additional amount of stock.

Portfolio Insurance

- I manage an S&P Index portfolio that has market value $100 million.
- I want to provide a "floor" of $90 million on my portfolio over the next 12 months.
- I assume that the index return volatility is 18%, the dividend yield is 3%, and the interest rate is 4%, annual. I calculate the price of a 12-month put with strike $90 on index value $100 to be $2.59.
- To buy portfolio insurance, I need to buy $100 million/$100 or 1 million such puts at cost $2.59 million.
- The clever idea of LOR is to make this long position in puts synthetically.
- In this synthetic long position in puts, I sell some of my index holdings when the index price decreases. But, this is what everybody else wants to do!
- Hence the problems of LOR.
- Nowadays, long-dated puts (and calls) are traded at the CBOE. The actual CBOE contract, "LEAP", is not for index of value $100 but for index value 1396×100, (if the index today is at 1396). Thus, I have to buy 1 million/1396 = 716 contracts.

The General Binomial Model

- Let

  n = number of steps to the option maturity;

  j = number of **up** steps to the option maturity;

  $n - j$ = number of **down** steps to the option maturity.
- The number of paths to $C_{u^j d^{(n-j)}}$ is

$$\frac{n!}{j!(n-j)!},$$

  where

$$n! = n \cdot (n-1) \cdot (n-2) \cdots 2 \cdot 1.$$

- For the n-period case:

$$C = \left(\frac{1}{\bar{r}^n}\right) \sum_{j=0}^{n} \left(\frac{n!}{j!(n-j)!}\right) p^j (1-p)^{n-j} C_{u^j d^{(n-j)}}$$

$$= \left(\frac{1}{\bar{r}^n}\right) \sum_{j=0}^{n} \left(\frac{n!}{j!(n-j)!}\right) p^j (1-p)^{n-j} \max[0, u^j d^{(n-j)} S - K].$$

- If we choose u and d carefully as n increases, in the limit as n increases this expression becomes the BSM formula for pricing a European call.
- You do not need to know the formulae on this page!

Chapter 8

Using the Binomial Model

Agenda

- Introduction
- Dividends
- Early exercise
- Time-dependent binomial trees
- Choosing the inputs to the binomial model
- Is the binomial model with $d = 1/u$ reasonable?
- The log-normal model of stock returns
- Lessons from long-term capital management (LTCM)

Introduction

We have seen how to construct a binomial model and how to price European calls and puts on non-dividend-paying stocks. Now we focus on how to extend and implement the model.

First, we show how to extend the binomial model to allow for dividends, early exercise of American options, and time-dependent binomial trees.

Second, we explain how to calibrate the binomial model: How to choose the parameters u, d, and q to match the statistical properties of the underlying security.

Third, we explain that our particular way of choosing the parameters u and d imply that the stock price is log-normal. We point out that this model has limitations as it ignores stochastic volatility and jumps in the price. Finally, we elaborate on the log-normal model of stock returns.

Dividends

- **Example**: Suppose that the IBM current stock price is 50. IBM will pay a $10 dividend in one month. The price rises or falls by 20% each month. The monthly *simple* interest rate is 10%. Price a two-month *European* call option with strike price 40.
- We draw a two-stage binomial tree as follows. Note that the nodes do not recombine after the dividend. Note also that, after the first month, it is the post-dividend price that rises or falls by 20% over the following month.

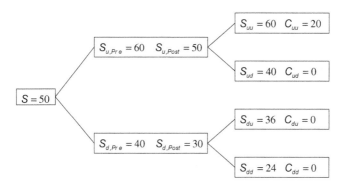

- Given $\bar{r} = 1.1, u = 1.2, d = 0.8$, we calculate the risk-adjusted probability as we did earlier:

$$p = \frac{\bar{r} - d}{u - d} = \frac{(1.1 - 0.8)}{(1.2 - 0.8)} = 0.75.$$

- The call prices one month from now are:

$$C_u = \frac{pC_{uu}}{\bar{r}} = \frac{0.75 \times 20}{1.1} = 13.64, C_d = 0.$$

- We calculate the call price today as follows:

$$C = \frac{p^2 C_{uu}}{\bar{r}^2} = \frac{0.75^2 \times 20}{1.1^2} = 9.30.$$

- The call delta now is:

$$\Delta = \frac{13.64 - 0}{60 - 40} = 0.68.$$

- To make a synthetic call, we buy fraction 0.68 of a share of stock and borrow $0.68 \times 50 - 9.30 = \$24.70$.

Early Exercise

- The binomial model is also useful for dealing with the possibility of early exercise. The basic approach is to work backwards through the binomial tree, deciding at each node whether to exercise or wait.
- Consider an *American* call on the same stock:

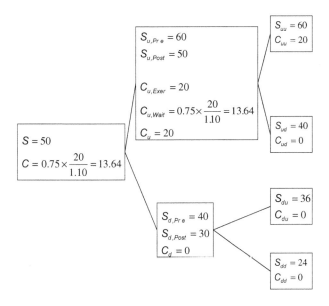

- Note that we use the pre-dividend price to determine the exercise value of a call at each node.
- If we were pricing a put, we would use the post-dividend price to determine the exercise value of a put.
- The hedge ratio of the American call is:

$$\Delta = \frac{20 - 0}{60 - 40} = 1.$$

- We make a synthetic American call by buying one share of stock and borrowing $1 \times 50 - 13.64 = \$36.36$.

Time-Dependent Binomial Trees

- Within the binomial model, it is easy to allow u, d, and $\bar{r}$ to change as long as they are only a function of S and t.

- The approach is the same as before: At each node we have parameters u and d, which may differ from the parameters at the other nodes. We calculate the risk-adjusted probability at each node and work backwards from the end of the tree, valuing the option at each node.

- Later on, we shall see that the parameters u and d are functions of the stock return volatility. If the volatility is a function of the stock price, so are the parameters u and d.

- In general, it is much harder to deal with the case where u and d are not exclusively functions of S and t. They do not fit easily into the binomial framework. We discuss these issues later on in the context of *stochastic volatility* and *jumps*.

Choosing the Inputs to the Binomial Model

- We divide the time between 0 and T into n steps, each of length T/n. We pick u, d, and q (yes, q the *real* probability) for each step so that the sum of the continuously compounded return from the n steps have the target mean and variance.
- The continuously compounded stock return for one step is:

$$\ln\left(\frac{S(t_i)}{S(t_{i-1})}\right) = \begin{cases} \ln(u) \text{ with probability } q \\ \ln(d) \text{ with probability } 1-q \end{cases}.$$

- The mean of the return for one step is:

$$E\left[\ln\left(\frac{S(t_i)}{S(t_{i-1})}\right)\right] = q\ln(u) + (1-q)\ln(d).$$

- The variance of the return for one step is:

$$\text{var}\left[\ln\left(\frac{S(t_i)}{S(t_{i-1})}\right)\right] = q\big[\ln(u) - \{q\ln(u) + (1-q)\ln(d)\}\big]^2$$

$$+ (1-q)\big[\ln(d) - \{q\ln(u) + (1-q)\ln(d)\}\big]^2$$

$$= q(1-q)\left[\ln\left(\frac{u}{d}\right)\right]^2.$$

- We assume that the return in each step is *independent* of previous stock return realizations and has annualized mean μ and annualized variance (squared volatility) σ^2.
- We choose u, d, and q to match the mean return over the interval T/n. Later on, we show that the mean return over the interval T/n is $\mu \times \left(\frac{T}{n}\right)$. Therefore,

$$q\ln(u) + (1-q)\ln(d) = \mu \times \left(\frac{T}{n}\right).$$

- We also choose u, d, and q to match the variance of the return over the interval T/n. Later on, we show that the return variance over the interval T/n is $\sigma^2 \times \left(\frac{T}{n}\right)$. Therefore,

$$q(1-q)\left[\ln\left(\frac{u}{d}\right)\right]^2 = \sigma^2 \times \left(\frac{T}{n}\right).$$

- Note that we have two equations for three unknowns (u, d, and q), so we have one extra degree of freedom.
- Let us set $d = 1/u$. Later on, we investigate the implications of this choice.
- With our choice $d = 1/u$, the solution is:

$$\ln(u) = \sigma\sqrt{\frac{T}{n}}\left(1 + \frac{\mu^2 T}{\sigma^2 n}\right)^{\frac{1}{2}} \approx \sigma\sqrt{\frac{T}{n}},$$

$$\ln(d) = -\sigma\sqrt{\frac{T}{n}}\left(1 + \frac{\mu^2 T}{\sigma^2 n}\right)^{\frac{1}{2}} \approx -\sigma\sqrt{\frac{T}{n}}$$

and

$$q = \frac{1}{2} + \frac{\mu}{2\sigma}\sqrt{\frac{T}{n}}\left(1 + \frac{\mu^2 T}{\sigma^2 n}\right)^{-\frac{1}{2}} \approx \frac{1}{2} + \frac{\mu}{2\sigma}\sqrt{\frac{T}{n}}.$$

- The approximation is reasonable. For example, for $\mu = 0.10$ per year, $\sigma = 0.30$ per year, $n = 100$ (100 steps), and $T = 1/12$ (a one-month option), we have $\mu^2 T/\sigma^2 n \approx 0.0001$ which is much smaller than 1.
- Finally, we write $u \approx e^{\sigma\sqrt{T/n}}, d \approx e^{-\sigma\sqrt{T/n}}$.
- In words: *u is the exponentiated value of the volatility over one step of the binomial tree.*
- For plain vanilla options we obtain a good approximation by using 30 or 60 steps.
- For exotic options such as "up-and-out" calls, we need to use many more steps.
- How do we set the gross risk-free rate per step, $\bar{r}$? Let $\bar{R}$ be the gross return *per year*, say 10%, $\bar{R} = 1.10$. If there are n steps between time 0 and T, with T measured in years, the time between steps is T/n and $\bar{r}$ (one plus the interest rate per step) is $\bar{r} = (\bar{R})^{T/n}$.
- If, instead, we are given the annual c.c. risk-free return, r, then $\bar{r} = e^{r \times \frac{T}{n}}$.
- Finally, the risk-adjusted probability is $p = \frac{\bar{r}-d}{u-d}$.

Is the Binomial Model with $d = 1/u$ Reasonable?

- There are four limitations to the model:
  1. The model does not allow for stock price jumps. To see this, note that for large n, $u \approx 1$, and $d \approx 1$.
  2. The model assumes that volatility is constant. Later on we address stochastic volatility.
  3. The assumption of the independence of stock returns rules out momentum.
  4. The model implies that the stock price is log-normal, yet we often observe fat-tailed stock return distributions — Black Swans. We explore this point in detail below.

- In the limit, as the number of steps in the tree goes to infinity, the probability distribution of the final stock price becomes log-normal — though we don't need very many steps to get accurate options prices. Let us understand why.

Justification of the Mean and Variance of the Return Over One Step of the Binomial

- Write the *arithmetic* stock return over one year (say, 240 trading days) as:

$$\frac{S(240)}{S(0)} = \frac{S(1)}{S(0)} \times \frac{S(2)}{S(1)} \times \cdots \times \frac{S(240)}{S(239)}.$$

- Take the logarithm of both sides to obtain the continuously-compounded return as:

$$\ln\left(\frac{S(240)}{S(0)}\right) = \ln\left(\frac{S(1)}{S(0)}\right) + \ln\left(\frac{S(2)}{S(1)}\right) + \cdots + \ln\left(\frac{S(240)}{S(239)}\right).$$

- The assumption that *the daily expected return is constant* implies that

$$E\ln\left(\frac{S(240)}{S(0)}\right) = E\ln\left(\frac{S(1)}{S(0)}\right) + E\ln\left(\frac{S(2)}{S(1)}\right)$$

$$+ \cdots + E\ln\left(\frac{S(240)}{S(239)}\right) = 240 \times E\ln\left(\frac{S(1)}{S(0)}\right)$$

or, equivalently

$$E\ln\left(\frac{S(1)}{S(0)}\right) = \frac{1}{240} \times E\ln\left(\frac{S(240)}{S(0)}\right).$$

This provides the intuition for setting the mean return over one step of the binomial as $\mu \times \left(\frac{T}{n}\right)$.

- The assumption that *the daily expected return is uncorrelated and the daily variance is constant* implies that

$$\operatorname{var}\ln\left(\frac{S(240)}{S(0)}\right) = \operatorname{var}\ln\left(\frac{S(1)}{S(0)}\right) + \operatorname{var}\ln\left(\frac{S(2)}{\tilde{S}(1)}\right)$$

$$+\cdots+ \operatorname{var}\ln\left(\frac{S(240)}{\tilde{S}(239)}\right)$$

$$= 240 \times \operatorname{var}\ln\left(\frac{S(1)}{S(0)}\right)$$

or, equivalently

$$\operatorname{var}\ln\left(\frac{S(1)}{S(0)}\right) = \frac{1}{240} \times \operatorname{var}\ln\left(\frac{S(240)}{S(0)}\right).$$

This provides the intuition for setting the return variance over one step of the binomial as $\sigma^2 \times \left(\frac{T}{n}\right)$.

- Caution: μ, σ, and T should be measured in the same time unit.
- **Example 1**: If the continuously-compounded return has mean 8% per year and volatility 40% per year, then the monthly mean return is $(1/12) \times 0.08$ and the monthly volatility is $\sqrt{1/12} \times 0.40$.
- **Example 2**: If the continuously-compounded return has mean 1% per month and volatility 7% per month, then the two-month mean return is 2×0.01 and the two-month volatility is $\sqrt{2} \times 0.07$.

The Log-Normal Distribution

- By the *Central Limit Theorem* (you do not need to know this technical staff for the final exam), if u and d go to 1 "fast enough" as $n \to \infty$, then $\ln(\tilde{S}(T)/S(0))$ converges to a normally distributed random variable.
- Our binomial tree with $d = 1/u$ and many steps satisfies this technical condition and implies that $\ln(\tilde{S}(T)/S(0))$ is normally distributed.
- If $\ln(\tilde{S}(T)/S(0))$ is normally distributed we say that $\tilde{S}(T)/S(0)$ and $\tilde{S}(T)$ are *log-normally distributed.*
- That the stock price is log-normally distributed is merely a model assumption and has its limitations. Later on, we model the stock price more realistically to allow for *stochastic volatility* and *jumps* in the stock price.

Example of a normal distribution

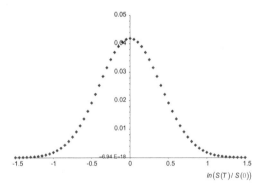

Example of a log-normal distribution

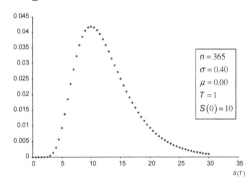

Lessons from Long-Term Capital Management (LTCM)

- LTCM came to existence in 1994 and was bankrupt in 1998. Read the posted articles and the discussion in Marthinsen.
- Liquid markets for borrowing and trading become illiquid at those rare but crucial times when you need to borrow or trade fast.
- Leverage magnifies profits but also magnifies losses and excessive reliance on liquid markets.
- Uncorrelated returns across markets normally allow a hedge fund to diversify its portfolio. However, at times of financial crisis, these returns may become highly correlated.
- Convergence trades may diverge for extended periods of time before they ultimately converge: Unrealistically large yield spreads widened during the 1997 Asian currency crisis and the 1998 Russian bond default.
- Modeling risk through Value-at-Risk (VaR) fails if we improperly model rare events, jumps, and correlations.
- Vultures prey on big wounded players by gaming against them.

Assignment 5

1. (a) NanoTech (NT), a dominant PC software company, intends to make a tender offer for Ratiocyn, a rapidly growing developer of personal tax software. However, because of concerns about predative behavior of NT, it is possible that the antitrust division of the US Department of Justice will decide that NT may not acquire Ratiocyn. The Justice Department will announce its decision in exactly two months. NT has announced that, if it is allowed to pursue the tender offer, it will make a cash offer of $60 per share for all outstanding shares. This is a very good offer, as the market value of Ratiocyn, should the tender offer not be allowed to go through, will fall immediately to $30 per share. The market value of Ratiocyn is currently $43 per share. The tender offer is structured in such a way that, upon approval of the Justice Department, a Ratiocyn holder could tender and immediately receive $60 per share. The monthly, continuously compounded risk-free rate for borrowing and lending is 1.00%.

   (a) Find the value of a call option on Ratiocyn, with strike price of 50, which will mature just after the justice department ruling is to be announced. (Hint: Set $S_u = 60$ and $S_d = 30$.)

   (b) Solve for the risk-adjusted probability that the justice depart ment will allow the tender offer to go through.

   (c) If the true probability of the tender offer going through is 50%, find the (monthly, simple) rate at which the market is discounting the cashflows from Ratiocyn common stock.

   (d) Now suppose a leak emerges from the Justice Department which shifts the true probability of a ruling in favor of NT to 40%, but the rate at which the market discounts the expected future cashflows from Ratiocyn remains the same as in (c). Does the price of the call change? If so, what is the new value?

   (e) We know that the true probability of an up or down move is "not important" for pricing options. How do you reconcile this with your answer in (d)?

2. Intel is currently trading at $50. Over each of the next two months, Intel will either move up by 25% or down by 20%.

Each month, the probability that Intel will move up is 60%. The simple monthly (and monthly compounded) risk-free rate is 1.00%. Further, assume that in exactly one month, Intel will pay a dividend equal to 10% of the price of Intel stock at that time. For example, if the price of Intel is $45 in one month, the dividend will be $4.50.

(a) Write out a two-month, two-period binomial tree for the stock price of Intel (i.e., one month per branch). Write down the binomial model parameters u, d, r, p, and q.

(b) Use the binomial method to find the price of a two-month American call on Intel with $K = 50$.

(c) Use the binomial method to find the price of a two-month American put on Intel with $K = 50$.

(d) Use the binomial method to find the price of a European "binary" option which pays off $100 if the price of Intel is greater than or equal to $50 in two months, and pays off zero otherwise.

(e) How many shares would you purchase and how much would you borrow/lend today to replicate the European binary option in (d)? What is the total cost of this replicating portfolio?

3. Assume that the annualized, continuously compounded return on Ford stock is normally distributed with mean 0.18 and standard deviation 0.4. In addition, the annualized, continuously compounded risk-free rate is 4%. The current price of Ford stock is $50. Assume that no dividends are paid on the Ford stock over the next nine months.

(a) Find the values of u, d, r, and p for a three-period binomial that you may use to price a nine-month option.

(b) Using a three-period binomial model, find the price of a nine-month European put option on Ford with a strike price of 60.

(c) Using the same model (a three-period binomial model) find the price of a nine-month American put option on Ford with a strike price of 60.

(d) At the start of the tree (i.e., today) what are Δ and L for the portfolio that replicates the American put option?

(e) Assuming that the stock price moves up over the first three months, determine how the composition of the replicating portfolio would change. That is, how many additional shares would you buy/sell and how much additional cash would you borrow/lend? What is the net cost of these two transactions?

(f) Using the appropriate put-call parity equation, find the price of an American call option on Ford with nine months to maturity, and with a strike price of 60. *Do not work out the binomial tree for the call.* Explain why you used this version of put-call parity.

4. The current stock price of Hale Umbrellas is $20. The volatility of the stock return on this consumer products company moves inversely with the stock price:

$$\sigma/month = \frac{2}{S}.$$

For example, the current standard deviation is 10% (2/20) per month. The interest rate (simple) is 1% per month. If Hale will not pay dividends this year, estimate the value of an American call option with a strike price of $20 and a time to expiration of two months. Use the binomial approach with two periods. (When you use the formula in Lecture Note 8, please use month as your time unit, instead of years.) Would the value of the call be higher or lower if the volatility were always 10% per month?

5. Explain in your own words in what sense the binomial model (as opposed to the trinomial model) has built into it the assumption that the market is *liquid*. Present examples where it is potentially disastrous to assume that the market is liquid.

6. Explain why a dense binomial tree (meaning, n large) calibrated as $u = d^{-1} = e^{\sigma\sqrt{T/n}}$ effectively rules out jumps in the stock price process. Present examples where it is potentially disastrous to rule out jumps.

Chapter 9

The Black–Scholes–Merton Option Pricing Formula

Introduction

- We introduce the celebrated Black–Scholes–Merton (BSM) option pricing equation for European calls and puts. The model was developed by Fischer Black and Myron Scholes, along with Robert Merton. It is referred to as the "Black–Scholes" model or as the "Black–Scholes–Merton" model. We refer to it as the BSM model.

- On the course web site you will find the original 1973 paper by Fischer Black and Myron Scholes. Through JSTOR, you may also read 25-year perspectives by Myron Scholes at http://www.jstor.org/stable/116839 and Robert Merton at http://www.jstor.org/stable/116838.

- We state the assumptions underlying the BSM model, discuss the intuition of its derivation, interpret it, and provide an example.

- We extend the BSM equation to allow for stocks that pay dividends, either a known amount or a known yield. The extended formula for European calls on stocks with a known dividend yield can also be used to price options on stock indices and currencies.

The BSM Model Assumptions

- **The market is frictionless.**

Same as in the binomial model: No taxes, liquid market, no transaction fees, no restrictions on short sales, same borrowing and lending rates.

- **It is feasible to trade continuously or "as fast as information arrives in the market".**

The counterpart in the binomial model is that it is feasible to trade at each node of the binomial tree or "as fast as information arrives in the market". This property of the market relates to liquidity.

- **The market is complete.**

The counterpart in the binomial model is that stock price paths are described by binomial trees as opposed to trees with three or more branches. The important implication of this assumption is that we can make a synthetic derivative by using the stock and the bond alone. This property of the market also relates to liquidity.

- **The stock returns are identically and independently distributed (i.i.d.).**

This corresponds to the assumption on a binomial tree that the "u" and "d" are the same at all branches of the tree.

➤ We assume constant volatility.
➤ We rule out momentum.

- **The stock price is log-normally distributed.**

This corresponds to the assumption $d = 1/u$ on a binomial tree with many steps. It means that the continuously-compounded return over any period is normally distributed:

$$\ln\left(\frac{S(t_2)}{S(t_1)}\right) \sim N(\mu(t_2 - t_1), \sigma^2(t_2 - t_1)).$$

➤ A binomial tree with $d = 1/u$ implies that as the number of steps on the tree goes to infinity, the probability distribution of the final stock price becomes log-normal.

➤ We disallow stock price jumps.

• **The interest rate is constant.**

This is not a critical assumption because short-dated stock option prices are insensitive to the interest rate. It is a critical assumption for long-dated options.

The BSM Dynamic Trading Strategy

- In the context of the binomial model, we illustrated how we can replicate the final time-T payoff of a European call option by purchasing a portfolio of stocks and risk-free bonds at time $t = 0$, and dynamically trading the portfolio until time T.

- Black and Scholes' (1973) paper shows that, under the BSM assumptions, we can do the same: Replicate the final time-T payoff of a European call option by purchasing a portfolio of stocks and risk-free bonds at time $t = 0$, and dynamically trading the portfolio until time T.

- Therefore, the value of the European call must equal the value of the replicating portfolio at time $t = 0$.

- We do not derive the BSM pricing equation. However, in a binomial tree with $d = 1/u$ (the assumption that leads to a log-normal stock price as the number of steps increases), the European call price tends to a rather simple expression, *the BSM pricing equation*, as the number of steps increases.

The BSM Pricing Equation

- In the special case of zero dividends, the BSM price of a European call option is:

$$c(S, K, t = 0, T, r, \sigma) = SN(d_1) - Ke^{-rT}N(d_2),$$

where

$$d_1 = \frac{\ln(S/Ke^{-rT})}{\sigma\sqrt{T}} + \frac{\sigma\sqrt{T}}{2} = \frac{\ln(S/K) + rT + \sigma^2 T/2}{\sigma\sqrt{T}},$$

$$d_2 = d_1 - \sigma\sqrt{T} = \frac{\ln(S/Ke^{-rT})}{\sigma\sqrt{T}} - \frac{\sigma\sqrt{T}}{2}$$

$$= \frac{\ln(S/K) + rT - \sigma^2 T/2}{\sigma\sqrt{T}}.$$

- $N(x)$ is the cumulative normal distribution from $-\infty$ to x.
- The inputs to the BSM pricing equation are:

  ➤ The current stock price, S;
  ➤ The exercise price, K;
  ➤ The time to expiration, T;
  ➤ The volatility, σ;
  ➤ The c.c. interest rate, r.

- Note that *the expected return on the stock is not an input,* which is what we would expect based on our analysis of the binomial model.
- The simplest way to price a European put is to apply the BSM equation to price first the European call and then apply the put-call parity.
- Others prefer to combine the two steps in one as follows:

$$p(S, K, t = 0, r, \sigma)$$
$$= Ke^{-rT} - S + SN(d_1) - Ke^{-rT}N(d_2)$$
$$= Ke^{-rT}[1 - N(d_2)] - S[1 - N(d_1)]$$
$$= Ke^{-rT}N(-d_2) - SN(-d_1).$$

Here we use the fact that the standard normal distribution is symmetric and, therefore, $1 - N(x) = N(-x)$.

Interpretation of $N(d_1)$

- The hedge ratio of a call option is the derivative of the call price with respect to the stock price, keeping everything else constant:

$$\Delta_c = \frac{\partial c}{\partial S} = \frac{\partial \left[SN(d_1) - Ke^{-rT}N(d_2) \right]}{\partial S} = N(d_1).$$

- The calculation of the partial derivative above yields additional terms which cancel and we are left with $N(d_1)$.
- Thus $N(d_1)$ is the hedge ratio of a European call: The fraction of a share that we buy in the replicating portfolio today (at time $t = 0$).
- *Caution*: Traders approximate the probability that the call is ITM at maturity by its delta,

$$N(d_1) = N\left(\frac{\ln(S/K) + rT + \sigma^2 T/2}{\sigma\sqrt{T}} \right).$$

The correct probability that the call is ITM at maturity is:

$$N\left(\frac{\ln(S/K) + \mu T}{\sigma\sqrt{T}} \right),$$

where μ is the annualized c.c. expected rate of return on the stock.

Interpretation of $N(d_2)$

- $e^{-rT}KN(d_2)$ is the amount that we borrow in the replicating portfolio today. This is equivalent to L in the binomial method.
  - ➤ Just as in the binomial case, the value of the call option must be the cost of the replicating portfolio, $c = \Delta_c S - L = \Delta_c S - e^{-rT}KN(d_2)$.
- $N(d_2)$: The *risk-adjusted* probability that the call is ITM at maturity.
- We can apply the above interpretation to find the price of a *digital option* that pays off \$1 if the stock price is greater than K at maturity and zero otherwise. Its price is $e^{-rT}N(d_2)$.

- Interpretation of the BSM equation for deep ITM calls. As the stock price increases, both d_1 and d_2 increase, $N(d_1) \approx 1$, $N(d_2) \approx 1$, and $c \approx S - Ke^{-rT}$, the value of a forward position past initiation with delivery price K.

Example on the BSM equation

- We are given:

  $S = 60$;
  $r = 0.0862$, annualized, c.c.;
  $K = 65$;
  $\sigma = 0.30$ (annual);
  $T = 0.5$ years.
- We calculate $\sigma\sqrt{T} = 0.2123$ and

$$e^{-rT}K = 0.9578 \times 65 = 62.26.$$

- The European call price is:

$$c(S, K, t = 0, r, \sigma) = SN(d_1) - Ke^{-rT}N(d_2)$$
$$= 60N(d_1) - Ke^{-rT}N(d_2),$$
$$d_1 = \frac{\ln(S/Ke^{-rT})}{\sigma\sqrt{T}} + \frac{\sigma\sqrt{T}}{2}$$
$$= \frac{\ln(60/62.26)}{0.2123} + \frac{0.2123}{2} = -0.068,$$
$$N(d_1) = N(-0.068) = 1 - N(0.068)$$
$$= 1 - 0.527 = 0.473,$$
$$d_2 = d_1 - \sigma\sqrt{T} = -0.068 - 0.2123 = -0.280,$$
$$N(d_2) = N(-0.280) = 1 - N(0.280)$$
$$= 1 - 0.6103 = 0.390,$$
$$C = 60N(d_1) - 62.26\,N(d_2)$$
$$= 60 \times 0.473 - 62.26 \times 0.390 = 4.11.$$

- To make a synthetic call, buy fraction 0.473 of a share and borrow $62.26 \times 0.390 = 24.28$.

Estimating the Volatility

- Most inputs are directly observable: S, K, T, r.
- The volatility is the one input that we have to estimate either from the time-series data or as "implied volatility".
- *Historical volatility*: Estimate the variance

$$\hat{\sigma}^2 = \frac{1}{n} \sum_{i=1}^{n} \left[\ln \left(\frac{S_{t-i}}{S_{t-i-1}} \right) \right]^2.$$

Then take the square root of the variance. This calculation assumes that the expected daily return is approximately zero, which is usually a good assumption.

- *Implied volatility*: The *implied volatility* (IV) of a call is defined as the volatility input to the BSM equation that yields a call price equal to the observed call price.

  ➤ We may use the IV of the ATM option.
  ➤ The VIX index is the weighted average of options of different moneyness on the S&P500 index.

- We extensively discuss implied volatility later on.

Options on Stocks with Known Dividends

- Consider a call on a stock which pays dividend D at time t_1, where $t < t_1 < T$. The European call is an option on the stock at time T, *after* the dividend has been paid.
- So the underlying asset is not the stock *per se*, but the stock minus the present value of the dividend.
- The present value of the time-T stock price after the dividend payment, which is $S(t) - \text{PV}(D)$.
- Note that this argument also works for multiple dividend payouts between t and T, as long as we know the present (time-t) value $\text{PV}(D)$ of all dividends between t and T.
- We calculate the value of the call option by substituting $S(t) - \text{PV}(D)$ for $S(t)$ in the BSM equation:

$$c(t) = [S(t) - \text{PV}(D)]N(d_1) - Ke^{-r\tau}N(d_2)$$

$$d_1 = \frac{\ln\left[\frac{S(t)-\text{PV}(D)}{Ke^{-r\tau}}\right]}{\sigma\sqrt{\tau}} + \frac{\sigma\sqrt{\tau}}{2}, \quad d_2 = d_1 - \sigma\sqrt{\tau},$$

where $\tau = T - t$ and $\text{PV}(D)$ is the present value of all future dividends between t and T.

- Be careful to substitute $S(t) - \text{PV}(D)$ for $S(t)$ in the d_1 and d_2 terms too.

Options on Stocks with Known Dividend Yield

- The same reasoning we used earlier in deriving the forward price on a stock with a continuous dividend yield δ can be used here to value a stock with a continuous proportional dividend payout per unit time.
- If we buy one share of stock at t and reinvest the dividends back into the share holdings, then we will have $e^{\delta\tau}$ shares of stocks at time $T(\tau = T - t)$.
- The call is on one share of stock at T. So the "underlying asset" here is not one, but rather fraction $e^{-\delta\tau}$ of a share of stocks at t.
- We thus adjust the BSM equation by substituting $S(t)e^{-\delta\tau}$ for $S(t)$:

$$c(t) = S(t)e^{-\delta\tau}N(d_1) - Ke^{-r\tau}N(d_2),$$

$$d_1 = \frac{\ln\left[\frac{S(t)e^{-\delta\tau}}{Ke^{-r\tau}}\right]}{\sigma\sqrt{\tau}} + \frac{\sigma\sqrt{\tau}}{2}$$

$$= \frac{\ln[S(t)/K] + (r - \delta)\tau}{\sigma\sqrt{\tau}} + \frac{\sigma\sqrt{\tau}}{2},$$

$$d_2 = d_1 - \sigma\sqrt{\tau}.$$

- Be careful to substitute $S(t)e^{-\delta\tau}$ for $S(t)$ in the d_1 and d_2 terms too.

Options on Currencies

A foreign currency with c.c. interest r_f on the foreign currency is analogous to a stock paying a known dividend yield $\delta = r_f$, and we value it exactly the same way.

$$c(t) = S(t)e^{-r_f\tau}N(d_1) - Ke^{-r\tau}N(d_2),$$

$$d_1 = \frac{\ln\left[\frac{S(t)e^{-r_f\tau}}{Ke^{-r\tau}}\right]}{\sigma\sqrt{\tau}} + \frac{\sigma\sqrt{\tau}}{2}$$

$$= \frac{\ln[S(t)/K] + (r - r_f)\tau}{\sigma\sqrt{\tau}} + \frac{\sigma\sqrt{\tau}}{2},$$

$$d_2 = d_1 - \sigma\sqrt{\tau}.$$

Chapter 10

Options on Futures

Introduction

- Let t be the current date.
- Let T' be the futures' maturity date.
- Let T be the expiration date of an option on the futures.
- Options on futures expire either on or before the futures' maturity date: $T \leq T'$.
- Options on futures are settled in cash, based on the futures price at the close for the day.
- If the option is European, the *cash* payoff at maturity T is:

$$\text{Call payoff} = \max[0, F(T_{\text{CLOSE}}, T') - K]$$
$$\text{Put payoff} = \max[0, K - F(T_{\text{CLOSE}}, T')].$$

- If the option is American, the *cash* payoff from exercising at time t is:

$$\text{Call payoff} = F(t_{\text{CLOSE}}, T') - K$$
$$\text{Put payoff} = K - F(t_{\text{CLOSE}}, T').$$

- Specifically, when you exercise an American call on the S&P 500 futures at time t, you get $F(t_{\text{CLOSE}}, T') - K$ credited to your margin account plus long futures on the index.

How Do We Price Options on Futures?

- JPMorgan constructs a portfolio (think of it as an ETF) with market value that tracks the futures price as follows:

  ➤ At the end of day t, JPMorgan buys one futures and places in a money market account $\$F(t, T')$. The value of the ETF is $\$F(t, T')$.

  ➤ At the end of day $t + 1$, JPMorgan gets one day of interest on $F(t, T')$ which pays out as dividend to the holders of the ETF.

  ➤ In addition, JPMorgan gets the principal $F(t, T')$, and the daily marking-to-market profit (or, loss) $F(t + 1, T') - F(t, T')$ from the futures contract.

  ➤ The principal $F(t, T')$ and the marking-to-market profit (or, loss) $F(t + 1, T') - F(t, T')$ sum to $\$F(t + 1, T')$.

  ➤ Finally, JPMorgan holds on to the futures contract, and places in a money market account $\$F(t + 1, T')$.

  ➤ Repeating this strategy every day, JPMorgan has constructed an ETF with market value that tracks the futures price and pays dividend yield r every day.

- Fischer Black pointed out that:

  An option on the futures can be thought of as an option on a tracking portfolio which has market value $\$F(t, T')$ and (fictitious) dividend yield r.

- Is it sometimes optimal to exercise an American call on futures early?
- Does Black's model apply to European options on both financial futures and commodity futures?
- Does Black's model apply if the underlying asset of the futures contract pays dividends, for example, a call option on the euro futures?
- When we use Black's model to calculate the price of an option on, say, pork belly futures, which volatility should we use: The volatility of the pork belly futures price, or the volatility of the spot pork belly price?

The Put-Call Parity for Options on Futures

- Our discussion suggests that the European put-call parity for options on futures is given by

$$c - p = e^{-r(T-t)}F(t,T') - e^{-r(T-t)}K.$$

- If the above is violated, there is arbitrage.
- Example. Suppose that

$$F(t,T') = 100, \quad K = 105, \quad c = 3.00, \quad p = 8.19, \quad r = 10\% \text{ c.c.}$$

Since

$$3.00 - 8.19 < e^{-0.10 \times 0.5}100 - e^{-0.10 \times 0.5}105,$$

there is arbitrage:

| Transaction | Cashflow now, t | Cashflow at the option expiration, T | |
		$F(T,T') \leq 105$	$F(T,T') > 105$
Buy call	-3.00	0	$F(T,T') - 105$
Write put	8.19	$-[105 - F(T,T')]$	0
Short forward	0	$-[F(T,T') - 100]$	$-[F(T,T') - 100]$
Lend $e^{-0.10\times0.5}(105 - 100)$	$e^{-0.10\times0.5}(100 - 105)$	$105 - 100$	$105 - 100$
Total	0.43	0	0

Pricing a European Call on the Futures with the BSM Formula

We want to find the price $c(0)$ today ($t = 0$) a European call of maturity T on a futures with maturity T' and price $F(0, T')$.

Substitute $F(0, T')e^{-rT}$ for $S(t)$, in the original BSM equation and obtain

$$c(0) = F(0, T')e^{-rT} N(d_1) - Ke^{-rT} N(d_2),$$

$$d_1 = \frac{\ln\left[\frac{F(0,T')e^{-rT}}{Ke^{-rT}}\right]}{\sigma\sqrt{T}} + \frac{\sigma\sqrt{T}}{2} = \frac{\ln[F(0, T')/K]}{\sigma\sqrt{T}} + \frac{\sigma\sqrt{T}}{2},$$

$$d_2 = d_1 - \sigma\sqrt{T}.$$

Example of Building a Binomial Tree for Futures

- Consider a stock with volatility $\sigma = 6.26\%$ per year and zero dividend. The interest rate is 20% c.c. per year. We want to build a binomial tree with $T = 6$ months and 50 steps.
- Calculate:

$$u = e^{\sigma\sqrt{T/n}} = 1.02, \qquad d = 1/u = 0.98,$$

$$\bar{r} = e^{r \times (T/n)} = 1.002, \qquad p = \frac{\bar{r} - d}{u - d} = 0.55.$$

- Build the stock tree:
  $S(0) = 100$ becomes either $1.02 \times 100 = 102$ or $0.98 \times 100 = 98$; and so on.
- Build the futures tree using the cost-of-carry formula:
  $F(0, T) = 100 \times (1.002)^{50} = 110.51$ becomes either $102 \times (1.002)^{49} = 112.49$ or $98 \times (1.002)^{49} = 108.08$; and so on.
- *Shortcut*: Note that over each step of the binomial the futures price either increases by the multiplicative factor $u/\bar{r}$ or decreases by the multiplicative factor $d/\bar{r}$. For example, we can obtain 112.49 as $110.51 \times 1.02/1.002$.

The VIX Index

- The VIX index is 100 times the forecast of the annualized 30-day volatility of the S&P500 index (SPX).
- It is based on the weighted average of the implied volatility of S&P500 index options with 1-month and 2-month expiration and wide range of moneyness.
- It is designed in a way that it is robust to whether the BSM pricing formula correctly prices options or not.

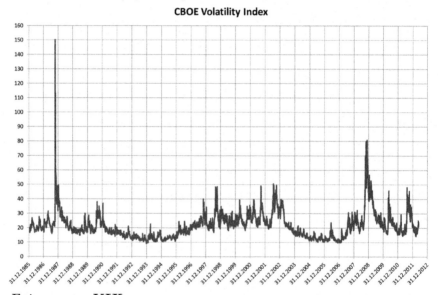

CBOE Volatility Index

Futures on VIX

- Futures on the VIX (ticker symbol: VX) are traded on the CBOE Futures Exchange (CFE) with contract size $1000 times VIX.
- Can we apply the cost-of-carry formula to relate the VIX to the VIX futures?
- Can we make a synthetic VIX futures by buying a straddle on the index?

Options on VIX Futures

- Options on the VIX futures (ticker symbol: VRO) are also traded.
- Can we apply the BSM formula to price the VIX futures options?
- In 2008, the CBOE launched another type of volatility options (RUH) based on the 3-month realized volatility on the S&P500 index.

Assignment 6

1. (*Getting familiar with BSM*)

(a) Consider a European call option and a European put option with the same strike price K on the same non-dividend-paying stock. Write down the explicit price of these two options using the BSM equation and show that these two prices satisfy the put-call parity.

(b) Do you expect the above-calculated European call and put prices from BSM to satisfy the put-call parity even without the above proof?

(c) Consider a European call option on a non-dividend-paying stock that is very deep in the money; that is, the current stock price is much larger than the strike price K. Use the BSM formula to show that the value of such a call option is approximately equal to the value of a forward contract on the stock with delivery price K and maturity T.

2. (*Plotting the BSM formula*) In Lecture Note 4, we showed the range of possible market prices for a European call option and a European put option on a non-dividend-paying stock, based on simple no-arbitrage arguments without making any assumption on how the stock price moves over time. Now that we have the BSM formula for these option prices, we can go back and plot the call option value and the put option value as a function of the current stock price by using Hull's software. Consider a European call option and a European put option, with the same strike $K = 100$, on a non-dividend-paying stock. Assume that $r = 5\%$ (annualized, c.c.), $T - t = 1$ year, and volatility 30% per year.

(a) Using the BSM formula and Hull's software, plot the value of the call option as a function of the current stock price. On the plot, indicate the no-arbitrage boundaries.

(b) Using the BSM formula and Hull's software, plot the value of the put option as a function of the current stock price. On the plot, indicate the no-arbitrage boundaries.

(c) Did the calculated values of the deep-in-the-money and deep-out-of-the-money call and put options turn out to be what you expected?

3. An interesting question is how many tree steps are necessary to properly price an option. To investigate this, assume that Intel has a current price of $50 and a volatility of 25% per year, and that the interest rate is 10% per year. Using Hull's software, calculate the value of a European call option with an exercise price of 50 and time to expiration two months, using binomial trees with steps of 2, 5, 10, 50, 100, and 200. Plot the results. Calculate the price of the same option using the BSM formula and compare with the results from the binomial-tree model.

4. The CAD–USD spot exchange rate is 1.30 CAD/USD. Assume that the volatility of the exchange rate is 15% per year. The USD annualized c.c. interest rate is 4.60% and the CAD annualized c.c. interest rate is 6.60%. Calculate the USD value of a European option to buy 1,000,000 CAD at the price of 710,000 USD in 9 months.

5. The S&P100 index is currently trading at 600. Consider a two-stage binomial tree with the length of each stage equal to one month. We are given $u = 1.12, d = u^{-1}$, and the c.c. interest rate 1% per month.

   (a) Price a 2-month American put on the index with strike 610.
   (b) Consider a 6-month futures contract on the index. Build a 2-month futures price tree. Assume for simplicity that the index futures is marked to market monthly rather than daily.
   (c) Suppose that you want to hedge the American put in part (a) with the 6-month futures contract. Create a hedge portfolio and explain what actions you need to take in a month from now.
   (d) If the actual price of the put today is $27.15, what is the arbitrage profit today in trading one put? Explain how you lock in the arbitrage profit today and hedge your position.
   (e) Price a 2-month American put on the 6-month index futures. The strike price is 610. How does your answer differ from (a)? Explain.

6. Look up the prices of the nearest ATM June S&P500 index calls and the S&P500 index futures calls. Include with your assignment a copy of the web site from which you obtained the prices. [You may find the S&P500 index price on the CBOE web site or Yahoo! Finance; the S&P500 index option prices (SPX) on the CBOE web site; the index futures and options on futures on the CME web site by visiting CME — Products — S&P 500 — Delayed futures or Delayed options.]

(a) Prove that the two calls should have the same price, if they are both European.

(b) Now, recognize that the futures call is American and, therefore, should have a higher price than the index call that is European. Make reasonable assumptions about the inputs, employ Hull's software, and determine whether the quoted prices of these calls imply a profit opportunity.

7. Consider an at-the-money-forward European call on the stock. (This means that the strike equals the forward price on the stock, with delivery date the call's maturity.) Dividend at the constant dividend yield δ is paid on the stock.

(a) (*This part is optional*) A popular rule-of-thumb is that the price of the ATM-forward European call, as a fraction of the stock price, is approximately $\frac{\sigma\sqrt{T}}{2.5}$. Try to prove it by approximating the density of the normal distribution.

(b) (*This part is optional*) Another popular rule-of-thumb is that the delta of the ATM-forward European call is approximately $\frac{1}{2} + \frac{\sigma\sqrt{T}}{5}$. Try to prove it.

(c) Robinson was stranded on a barren island without power for his laptop and without the normal distribution tables. He used the above rules to calculate the price and delta of a 3-month, at-the-money-forward European call on a stock that has price $40 and annual volatility 15%. What numbers did he get?

(d) Ten years later, a passing ship rescued Rob. As a true Booth MBA, Rob immediately charged his laptop and calculated the BSM price and delta of the ATM-forward European call.

He tried a range of different values for the interest rate and the dividend yield. Verify, as Rob did, that his calculations in (c) were correct all along. (Rob was immensely relieved that he did not miss much over the previous ten years.)

8. (*This problem is optional. It illustrates Girsanov's Theorem, a result extensively used in the industry that allows us to estimate the vol from time-series data and then argue that the estimated volatility is the appropriate volatility for the risk-adjusted process.*)

   In Chapter 8, we were given the annualized c.c. mean return, μ, the annualized volatility, σ, and the time length of one binomial step, T/n.

   (a) State the implied values of u, d and the *real* probability, q.

   (b) Use the values of u, d and q, from (a) to calculate the volatility of the return over a period of length T/n. (You should find that the answer is σ, and this should not be surprising. You are simply reversing the steps in (a).)

   (c) Use the values of u, d and the c.c. risk-free rate, r, to calculate the *risk-adjusted* probability, p.

   (d) Now use the values of u, d and the *risk-adjusted* probability, p, from (c) (not the *real* probability, q), to calculate the volatility of the return over a period of length T/n. You should find again that the answer is σ, for large n, and this is very surprising. How do you interpret this result?

Chapter 11

Risk Management

Introduction

We study risk management from the perspective of an option trader. We first describe the risk characteristic of options, forwards, and futures in terms of the greeks: delta, gamma, theta, vega, and rho. We then show how to delta-hedge a portfolio and then increase the robustness of the hedge by gamma-hedging in addition to delta-hedging. We explore the concept of convexity and the linkage between the delta, gamma, and theta of a portfolio. Finally, we introduce the concept of Value-at-Risk (VaR).

Delta

- Let $V(S)$ be the price of a call, put, or, more generally, a portfolio of European or American derivatives, all written on the same underlying security that has price S.
- The delta of the portfolio is defined as $\Delta = \partial V / \partial S$: The dollar increase in the portfolio value when the price of the underlying security increases by \$1.
- The delta is the slope of the graph of V as a function of S.
- For a European call with either zero or fixed dividend,

$$\Delta_c = \frac{\partial c}{\partial S} = N(d_1) > 0.$$

- For a European call with dividend yield δ,

$$\Delta_c = \frac{\partial c}{\partial S} = e^{-\delta(T-t)} N(d_1) > 0.$$

- For a European put with either zero or fixed dividend,

$$\Delta_p = \frac{\partial p}{\partial S} = \Delta_c - 1 = N(d_1) - 1 < 0.$$

Proof: $p = c - [S - \text{PV}(D)] + \text{PV}(K)$. Differentiate with respect to S to get $\Delta_p = \frac{\partial p}{\partial S} = \Delta_c - 1$.

- For a European put with dividend yield δ,

$$\Delta_p = \frac{\partial p}{\partial S} = \Delta_c - e^{-\delta(T-t)} = e^{-\delta(T-t)} [N(d_1) - 1] < 0.$$

Proof: $p = c - e^{-\delta(T-t)} S + \text{PV}(K)$. Differentiate with respect to S to get $\Delta_p = \frac{\partial p}{\partial S} = \Delta_c - e^{-\delta(T-t)} = e^{-\delta(T-t)} [N(d_1) - 1]$.

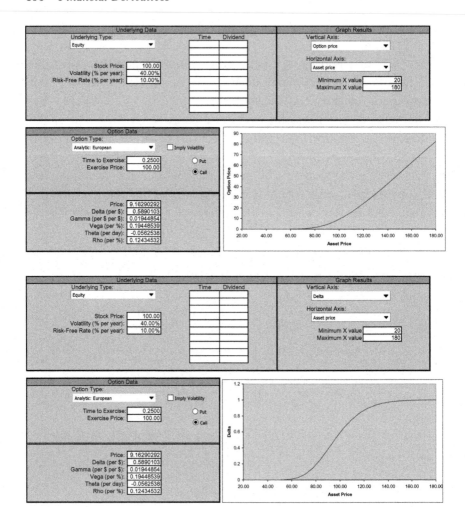

Gamma

- The gamma of the portfolio is defined as $\Gamma = \partial\Delta/\partial S$: The increase in the portfolio delta when the price of the underlying security increases by \$1.
- The gamma is the *convexity* of the graph of V as a function of S.
- The gamma is also the slope of the graph of Δ as a function of S.
- For European calls and puts, $\Gamma_c = \Gamma_p$, with or without dividends.
- Proof with fixed dividend: $p = c - [S - \mathrm{PV}(D)] + \mathrm{PV}(K)$. Differentiate twice with respect to S to get $\Gamma_c = \Gamma_p$.
- Proof with constant dividend yield: $p = c - e^{-\delta(T-t)}S + \mathrm{PV}(K)$. Differentiate twice with respect to S to get $\Gamma_c = \Gamma_p$.
- European and American calls and puts have positive gamma. Recall the graphs of these derivative prices as functions of the stock price.
- For very deep OTM or ITM calls, the gamma is close to zero. Likewise for puts.
- The gamma of a call or put peaks near the money. Delta-hedging a near-the-money call or put with the stock alone requires frequent re-hedging.

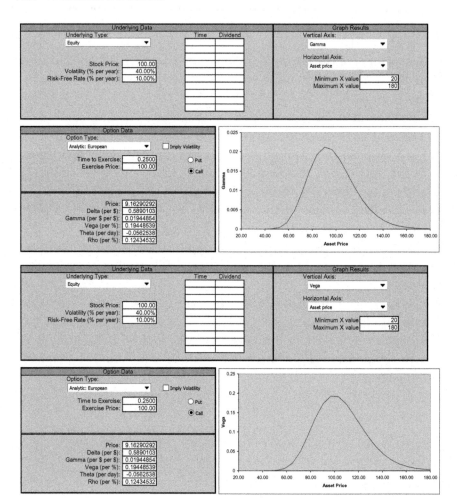

Vega

- The vega is the asset's increase in value when the volatility of the underlying security increases:

$$\nu = \frac{\partial V}{\partial \sigma}.$$

- Vega is an important parameter for options traders worried about changes in the volatility of the underlying stock.
- The vega of European and American calls and puts is positive.
- For very deep OTM or ITM calls, the vega is close to zero. Likewise with puts.
- The vega of a call or put peaks near the money.
- For European calls and puts, $\nu_c = \nu_p$, with or without dividends. To see this, differentiate the put-call parity with respect to the volatility.
- The vega and gamma of a European call or put are closely related:

$$\nu = \Gamma \times (T - t) \times \sigma \times S^2.$$

- Buying a portfolio with positive vega is "buying volatility". Typically we do this by buying a call and a put — a straddle.

Theta

- The theta is the increase in the asset's value as time elapses, while other things (like the stock price and volatility) remain constant: $\Theta = \frac{\partial V}{\partial t}$.
- The value of a call option on a non-dividend-paying stock decreases as time elapses both because the variance of the final price decreases and because the exercise price is less heavily discounted. Thus $\Theta_c < 0$.
- The fact that Θ_c is negative does not imply that the call price is expected to fall. The stock price is expected to rise over time — time is not the only thing that changes over time.
- For a European call on a stock with high dividend yield, theta can be positive or negative. Why?
- For an American call (with or without dividends), theta is negative. Why?
- For a European put (with or without dividends), theta can be positive or negative. Why?
- For an American put (with or without dividends), theta is negative. Why?

Call without Dividend

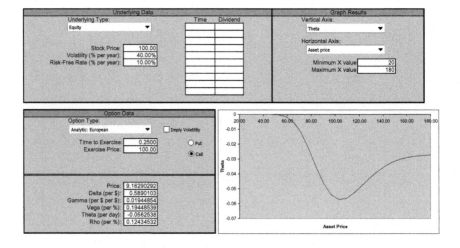

European Call with Dividend Yield

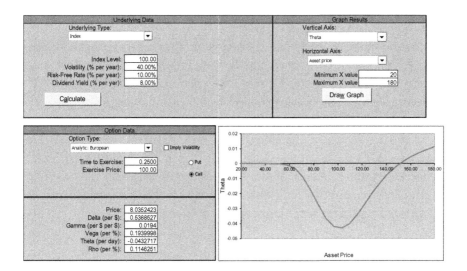

Rho

- The rho measures the increase in the asset's value when the interest rate increases: rho $= \frac{\partial V}{\partial r}$

- The rho of a European call is positive: in making a synthetic call we buy fraction of one share and *borrow* PV(K). If the interest rate increases (but the stock price and vol remain constant), PV(K) decreases and the cost of the synthetic call increases.

- The rho of an European put is negative: in making a synthetic put we short fraction of one share and *lend* PV(K). If the interest rate increases (but the stock price and vol remain constant), PV(K) decreases and the cost of the synthetic put decreases.

- Rho is important for long-dated options like ESOs (executive stock options) and warrants (calls issued by firms).

Greeks for Forward and Futures Contracts

- Recall from LN2 that the value of a forward contract past initiation is $\widehat{f}_t = [S(t) - \text{PV}(D)] - e^{-r(T-t)}K$ (or, $\widehat{f}_t = e^{-\delta(T-t)}S(t) - e^{-r(T-t)}K$). By differentiation, we obtained $\Delta_{\text{forw}} = \frac{\partial \widehat{f}_t}{\partial S(t)} = 1$ (or, $e^{-\delta(T-t)}$).

- Recall from LN2 that the value of a futures contract past initiation is $f_t = F(t,T) - F_{d-1} = [S(t) - \text{PV}(D)]e^{r(T-t)} - F_{d-1}$ (or, $f_t = e^{r(T-t)-\delta(T-t)}S(t) - F_{d-1}$). By differentiation, we obtained $\Delta_{\text{futures}} = e^{r(T-t)}$ (or, $e^{r(T-t)-\delta(T-t)}$).

- None of the above deltas is a function of the stock price. Therefore, *the gamma of forward and futures contracts is zero*, irrespective of whether the underlying stock pays no dividend, fixed dividend, or fixed dividend yield.

- The value of a forward or futures position is not a function of the stock volatility. Therefore, *the vega of forward and futures contracts is zero*.

- Can we use forward and futures to trade volatility?

General Approach to Risk Management

- We hedge a portfolio to keep its net value invariant to factors such as the stock price, volatility, and interest rate.
- Suppose that our portfolio is composed of three assets:

$$V = n_1 A_1 + n_2 A_2 + n_3 A_3,$$

where V denotes the value of the portfolio, n_i denotes the number of shares of the ith asset, and A_i denotes the market value of one share of the ith asset.

- Our objective in hedging is to pick the number of shares of these assets so that the value of the portfolio does not change when the factor x changes. That is, pick n_1, n_2, n_3 such that:

$$\frac{\partial V}{\partial x} = n_1 \frac{\partial A_1}{\partial x} + n_2 \frac{\partial A_2}{\partial x} + n_3 \frac{\partial A_3}{\partial x} = 0.$$

The value of the chosen portfolio then stays approximately constant as the factor x changes by a small amount.

- In general, we can hedge against $n - 1$ sources of uncertainty with n assets in the portfolio. For example, with three assets in the portfolio, we can choose n_1, n_2, and n_3 in a way such that the value of the portfolio does not change for small changes of the stock price *and* interest rate.

Example of Delta-Hedging

- A portfolio is *delta-hedged* (or, *delta neutral*) if the delta of the portfolio is zero. For example, take a portfolio of three assets and take the factor x to be the stock price.

$$\Delta_{\text{portfolio}} = \frac{\partial V}{\partial S} = n_1 \Delta_1 + n_2 \Delta_2 + n_3 \Delta_3 = 0$$

The value of this portfolio stays roughly constant for very small changes of S.

- **Example**: Suppose we wrote a 10-week call with strike 50 and now the stock price is 50, volatility 50% annual and c.c. interest rate 3% per year: $S = 50, K = 50, \tau = 10$ weeks, $\sigma = 0.5$, and $r = 0.03$.
- We find $\Delta_c(S, K, \tau, \sigma, r) = 0.554$.
- How many shares of stock should you buy so that you are delta hedged?
- Suppose we need to buy n_s shares. Since the Δ of a stock is 1, we choose n_s according to $n_s \times 1 + (-1) \times 0.554 = 0$.
- So we buy $n_s = 0.554$ shares of stock.
- Draw the value of the written call as a function of the stock price now.
- Draw the value of the 0.554 shares of stock as a function of the stock price now.
- Draw the value of the hedged portfolio as a function of the stock price now.

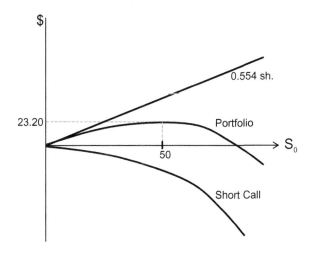

Robustness of the Delta-Hedge

- How robust is the portfolio value to stock price fluctuations?
- *Small change*: Let S increase from 50 to 51. Using BSM, we find that the value from the written call option decreases by $5.064 − $4.492 = $0.572, while the value of 0.554 shares of stock increases by $0.554. Our total loss is $0.572 − $0.554 = $0.018, which is small: less than 2 cents of loss for $1 increase in the stock price.
- What is the total gain/loss when S decreases to 49?
- *Large change*: Let S increase from 50 to 60. Using the BSM equation, we find that our value from the written call option decreases by $11.577 − $4.492 = $7.09, while the value of 0.554 shares of stock increases by $5.54. Our total loss is $7.09 − $5.54 = $1.55, which is large: about 16 cents of loss per $1 increase in stock price.
- What is the total gain/loss when S decreases to 40?
- We conclude that delta-hedging alone works badly for large changes in the stock price.
- Next, we consider gamma hedging on top of delta-hedging and demonstrate that it makes the hedge more robust.

Example of delta- and gamma-hedging

- A portfolio is *gamma-hedged* (or, *gamma-neutral*) if the Γ of the portfolio is zero, where

$$\Gamma_{\text{portfolio}} = \frac{\partial \Delta_{\text{portfolio}}}{\partial S}$$

$$= n_1 \frac{\partial \Delta_1}{\partial S} + n_2 \frac{\partial \Delta_2}{\partial S} + n_3 \frac{\partial \Delta_3}{\partial S}$$

$$= n_1 \Gamma_1 + n_2 \Gamma_2 + n_3 \Gamma_3.$$

- Can we use the stock to gamma-hedge an option?
- Let us now return to our example of a written ATM call option. We calculate its delta and gamma as $\Delta_1 = 0.554$ and $\Gamma_1 = 0.0361$.

- We use the stock and a second call on the same stock, with $K = 55$ and $\tau = 10$ weeks, to form a delta- and gamma-hedged portfolio.
- For this call, we calculate $\Delta_2 = 0.382$ and $\Gamma_2 = 0.0348$.
- Assume that we need n_s shares of stock and n_2 calls with strike 55.
- For delta-hedging, we require

$$n_s + 0.382\ n_2 - 0.554 = 0.$$

- For gamma-hedging, we require

$$0 + 0.0348\ n_2 - 0.0361 = 0.$$

- Solving these equations gives $n_s = 0.158$ and $n_2 = 1.037$.
- By how much does the portfolio value change, if S increases from 50 to 51? (Answer: The portfolio value increases by less than 0.1 cent.)
- By how much does the portfolio value change, if S increases from 50 to 60? (Answer: The portfolio value increases by 20 cents, much less (in absolute value) than the $1.55 decrease for our previous portfolio that was only delta-hedged.)
- To form the delta-hedged and gamma-hedged portfolio, we initially incur higher transaction costs than just delta-hedging the portfolio.
- However, the delta-hedged and gamma-hedged portfolio requires much less re-hedging in the future and cuts down on future transaction costs.
- Calculate the vega of the gamma-hedged portfolio and explain the result.

The Money Pump

- The earlier example of delta-hedging the call motivates the following attempt to build a money pump.
- Assemble the following portfolio:

  1. Buy one ATM call, paying $4.50.
  2. Short 0.554 shares, receiving $27.70.
  3. Deposit $23.20 in a money market account.

- The portfolio has zero value, zero delta, and positive gamma (positive convexity). The graph of the portfolio value as a function of the stock price is U-shaped, with the bottom of the U on the horizontal axis at $S = 50$.
- This portfolio appears to be a money pump: If the stock price increases, the portfolio value increases; if the stock price decreases, the portfolio value increases.
- What is the catch?
- To understand all this, we will digress to the foundations of the BSM pricing equation.
- Draw the value of the long call as a function of the stock price now.
- Draw the value of the 0.554 short shares of stock as a function of the stock price now.
- Draw the value of the hedged portfolio as a function of the stock price now.

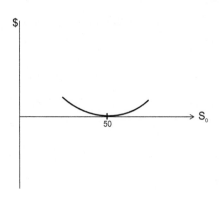

Relation between Delta, Gamma, and Theta

- Black and Scholes derived a partial differential equation (pde) and solved it to obtain the BSM pricing equation.
- We can write the Black–Scholes pde as follows:

$$\frac{1}{2}\sigma^2 S^2 \Gamma + (r - \delta)S\Delta + \Theta - rV = 0,$$

where V is the value of the claim.
- This relation between V, Δ, Γ, and Θ applies to European options, American options, and other derivatives on the stock as well.
- If V is not zero, we may rewrite this equation as follows:

$$r = \frac{\Theta + (r - \delta)S\Delta + \sigma^2 S^2 \Gamma/2}{V}.$$

- The left-hand side is the risk-adjusted total expected rate of return on the portfolio.
- Its components on the right-hand side are the risk-adjusted expected portfolio return due to:

  ➤ The passage of time, Θ
  ➤ The risk-adjusted stock price appreciation, $(r - \delta)S\Delta$
  ➤ The portfolio convexity, $\sigma^2 S^2 \Gamma/2$.

- For our money pump, $V = 0, \Delta = 0, \Gamma > 0$ and $\Theta < 0$, such that the risk-adjusted expected portfolio return is zero!
- Alternatively, we can "buy volatility" by buying one call and buying $-\Delta_c/\Delta_p$ puts. This portfolio is delta-neutral and has positive gamma and vega. This is a pure play on volatility.
- Traders typically buy volatility by buying a straddle. If we choose a call with delta approximately 0.5, the delta of the put is approximately $0.5 - 1 = -0.5$ and the straddle is approximately delta-neutral.

Value at Risk

- You cannot afford to be ignorant of Value-at-Risk (VaR) at your job-market interviews!
- VaR is the standard proposed by the Derivatives Policy Group for expressing the potential loss of a portfolio of assets.
- Let V_0 be the portfolio value today and V_T the portfolio value at, say, one day or 3 months from now.
- In-house portfolio managers typically use one-day VaR while banks typically use 3-month VaR.
- We say that the one-day VaR is L at the 99% confidence interval if the probability that $V_{\text{one day}} \leq V_0 - L$ is 1% or less. Illustrate on a graph.
- We say that the one-month VaR is L at the 95% confidence interval if the probability that $V_{\text{one month}} \leq V_0 - L$ is 5% or less.

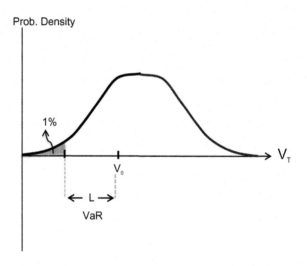

Chapter 12

Empirical Evidence and Fixes

You can observe a lot by watching — *Yogi Berra*

Agenda

- Introduction
- How to test the BSM pricing equation
- Stylized patterns of mispricing by the BSM pricing equation
- What are the market prices saying?
- Post-BSM models

Introduction

We ask how well the BSM equation does when compared to observed market prices of options. It turns out that, for S&P500 options, the BSM equation does significantly worse after the October 1987 market crash than before. We describe the stylized pattern of how the market option prices deviate from the BSM predictions. Finally, we discuss various ways in which one can improve upon the BSM equation.

How to Test the BSM Pricing Equation

- All input parameters for the BSM pricing equation are directly observable, except for the volatility.
- How do we test whether the BSM pricing equation works if we don't know the volatility?
- We can calculate the implied volatility (IV) from the market prices of options with different strike prices on the same stock.
- If the BSM pricing equation is correct, then these implied volatilities should be the same.
- In reality, however, options with different strike prices or maturities have different implied volatilities.
- The figures below are from my paper "Mispricing of S&P500 Index Options". The paper is posted under "Documents".

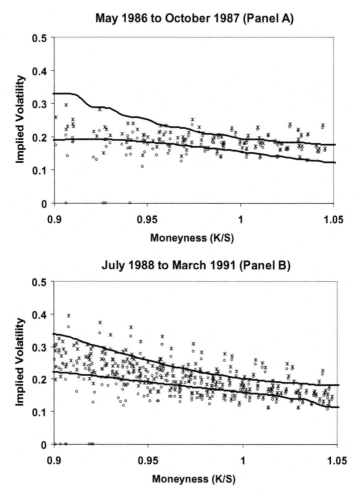

Fig. 1.   Bound violations over May 1986 to October 1987 and July 1988 to March 1991.

The observed bid (circles o) and ask (crosses x) call prices, as implied volatilities, are plotted as functions of the moneyness. The upper and lower option bounds are based on the index sample distribution 1972–2006, rescaled with the conditional volatility of the relevant panel. The transaction costs rate on the index is 50 bps.

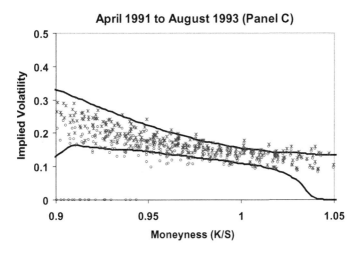

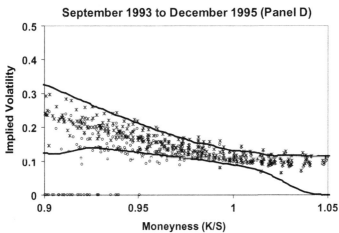

Fig. 2. Bound violations over April 1991 to August 1993 and September 1993 to December 1995.

The observed bid (circles o) and ask (crosses x) call prices, as implied volatilities, are plotted as functions of the moneyness. The upper and lower option bounds are based on the index sample distribution 1972–2006, rescaled with the conditional volatility of the relevant panel. The transaction costs rate on the index is 50 bps.

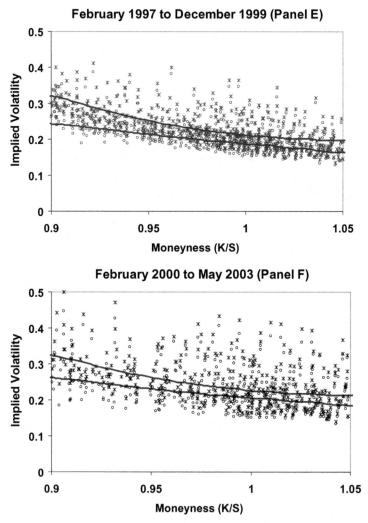

Fig. 3.   Bound violations over February 1997 to December 1999 and February 2000 to May 2003.

The observed bid (circles o) and ask (crosses x) call prices, as implied volatilities, are plotted as functions of the moneyness. The upper and lower option bounds are based on the index sample distribution 1972–2006, rescaled with the conditional volatility of the relevant panel. The transaction costs rate on the index is 50 bps.

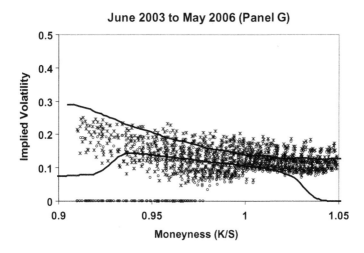

Fig. 4. Bound violations over June 2003 to May 2006.

The observed bid (circles o) and ask (crosses x) call prices, as implied volatilities, are plotted as functions of the moneyness. The upper and lower option bounds are based on the index sample distribution 1972–2006, rescaled with the conditional volatility of the relevant panel. The transaction costs rate on the index is 50 bps.

Stylized Patterns of Mispricing by the BSM

- If one uses the implied volatility (IV) for an ATM index option with a median maturity to price index options, then the mispricing pattern is:

  ➤ BSM underprices OTM puts. By the put-call parity, this is equivalent to saying that BSM underprices ITM calls.

  ➤ BSM overprices OTM calls. By the put-call parity, this is equivalent to saying that BSM overprices ITM puts.

  ➤ BSM underprices long-maturity ATM options and overprices short-maturity ATM options.

  ➤ The IV for ATM options is almost always higher than the actual volatility. This means that BSM overprices ATM options.

  ➤ There was no skew before the October 1987 crash.

What are the Market Prices Saying?

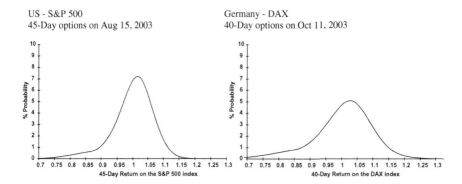

US - S&P 500
45-Day options on Aug 15, 2003

Germany - DAX
40-Day options on Oct 11, 2003

- Log-normality of prices (normality of log returns) is incorrect.
- The probability that the market goes down by a large amount is higher than that implied by the log-normal distribution.
- Therefore, OTM puts (and ITM calls) are priced higher than implied by the BSM equation.
- The probability that the stock market goes up by a large amount is less than that implied by the log-normal distribution.
- Therefore, OTM calls (and ITM puts) are priced lower than implied by BSM equation.

Post-BSM Models

- Post-BSM models either apply *ad hoc* fixes to the BSM equation or incorporate *stochastic volatility, negative price jumps,* and *positive volume jumps.*
- *Stochastic volatility*
  - ➤ Volume changes are typically *negatively* correlated with stock price changes.
  - ➤ A stock price drop leads to higher volume, which in turn leads to higher probability of extreme low prices.
  - ➤ A stock price increase leads to lower volume, which in turn leads to lower probability of extreme high prices.
- *Negative price jumps* increase the probability of extreme low prices.
- *Positive volatility jumps* appear to be even more important than stochastic volume and price jumps.
- Liquidity also affects option prices.
- In the paper "The Puzzle of Index Option Returns", posted under "Documents", I find that stochastic volume, price jumps, volume jumps, and liquidity explain the pricing of S&P 500 options.

A Simple Practitioners' Approach to Fix to the BSM Pricing Equation

- Record the shape of the "smile" from recent past observations.
- Assume that the same smile will persist in the future.
- Obtain the IV of the ATM option, via BSM.
- Use the graph to adjust for the bias of the BSM equation, given K/S. Plug the adjusted volatility in the BSM equation.
- We may use the adjusted BSM equation to calculate the greeks Δ, Γ, Θ. Also price OTC options.
- Market makers typically fit a smooth curve (for example, a quadratic or exponential curve) through the graph of IV. They judge options with IV above the curve as overpriced and options with IV below the curve as underpriced. They make a market in these options based on this information.

A More Sophisticated Practitioners' Approach

- View the IV as a *surface*, $\widehat{\sigma}(K/S, T)$, which is a function of two variables, moneyness (K/S) and time to expiration (T).
- Calculate the IV *surface*, $\widehat{\sigma}(K/S, T)$ from the prices of several exchange-traded options by regressing $\widehat{\sigma}(K/S, T)$ on the linear terms (K/S) and T and on the higher-order terms, $(K/S)^2$, $(K/S) \times T$, and T^2.
- We may use the surface to calculate the greeks Δ, Γ, Θ and also find overpriced and underpriced options; and price OTC options.
- The Holy Grail in the industry is the elusive goal of *predicting shifts* in the IV surface.

Financial Engineers' Fixes to the BSM Pricing Equation

- In post-BSM models, we incorporate *stochastic volatility, negative price jumps*, and *positive volume jumps*.
- We assume a time-series process for the stock price that incorporates jumps.
- We also assume a time-series process for the volatility that incorporates both a smooth component and jumps.
- We generalize the Black–Scholes partial differential equation (pde) $\frac{1}{2}\sigma^2 S^2 \Gamma + (r - \delta)S\Delta + \Theta - rV = 0$ to reflect the price jumps, stochastic volatility, and volatility jumps.
- The resulting pde is solved numerically. Financial engineers are experts in numerically solving such equations.

Assignment 7

This is a long assignment and Problems 4 and 5 are mini-projects that require advance planning.

1. You own a portfolio of options on Microsoft, Microsoft stock, and bonds. Currently, given the Microsoft stock price of $52, volatility 20% per year, and $r = 5.0\%$ (annualized, c.c.), your portfolio's Greeks are $\Delta = 50{,}000$, $\Gamma = 2{,}000/\$$, $\Theta = -\$500{,}000/\text{year}$, ν (vega) $= 50{,}000{,}000$ (or, $500{,}000$ per %), and ρ (rho) $= \$100{,}000$ (or, $\$1{,}000$ per %). One week later, the new market conditions are: Microsoft stock price $52.50, volatility 19%, and $r = 5.2\%$. What is the change in the value of your portfolio as the result of the change in (1) the stock price, (2) the volatility, and (3) the passage of time? What is the total change in the value of your portfolio?

2. A financial institution has the following portfolio of OTC options on euros:

Type	Number of options	Delta of option	Gamma of option (per $)	Vega of option (per %)
Exotic option	1,000	0.55	2.0	1.6
Exotic option	−500	0.60	0.7	0.6

A traded call option is available which has delta 0.6, gamma 0.3 (per $), and vega 0.2 (per %).

(a) What position in the traded call option and in euros would make the portfolio both gamma-neutral and delta-neutral?

(b) What position in the traded call option and in euros would make the portfolio both vega-neutral and delta-neutral?

3. Let the stock price be \$50. We are given the following information on the BSM prices of three European call options with 3 months to expiration:

K	45	50	55
C	6.86	3.60	1.61
Δ	0.83	0.60	0.35
Γ	0.034	0.052	0.049

(a) Write down the equations which one needs to solve to make a zero-cost, delta-neutral portfolio with a convexity of 0.05 by using the three types of calls. Do not solve these equations.

(b) Graph the value of this portfolio as a function of the stock price. (You only need to illustrate the functional form and you need not do any serious numerical calculations.)

(c) What is the portfolio's theta? Discuss the intuition behind the sign of the theta. (*Hint: Use the BSM differential equation.*)

4. (*Spreadsheet simulation of delta-hedging for a European call option.*) You are asked to simulate in an Excel Spreadsheet the delta-hedging of a call option, which was illustrated in Hull, Tables 18.2 and 18.3. The example for which you should produce the simulation is given in Chapter 11. Assume that you have written 1,000 contracts of these calls (100,000 calls), and that you need to hedge these calls by dynamically trading stocks and borrowing money through *weekly* rebalancing.

At week 0 (now), the stock price is 50. You construct your hedging portfolio according to the BSM equation by buying 55.40 thousand shares of the stock. For this problem, you do not need to specify how much you need to borrow since you will have a rolling borrowing account, as illustrated in Hull (see above). Given the following two scenarios of closing stock prices at the end of each of the next 10 weeks, please construct a spreadsheet (for each scenario) to show the following amounts for each week: (1) the delta of your portfolio; (2) the additional number of shares you need to purchase (or, sell) for the week; (3) the total number of shares you hold; (4) the marginal cost of your additional shares; (5) the cumulative amount of borrowing; and (6) the interest cost on your borrowing each week. Your spreadsheets should look like those in Hull, except that you have an additional column indicating how many total shares you have in your portfolio. The stock prices are:

Week	0	1	2	3	4	5	6	7	8	9	10
1st Scenario	50	52.5	51.5	52.5	54	57	55	59.25	59	61.5	63
2nd Scenario	50	53.5	48	47.5	44	46	41	42		38	37	34

Based on the spreadsheet simulation, compare the cost of replicating the options for each scenario with the $449.141 (thousand) value calculated by the BSM equation. (When you compare these values, please be aware that your cumulative cost is the total cost in 10 weeks of time while the option price is the current value.)

5. (*Calculating the volatility smile and trading on it*) Look at the closing prices of the March 2014 S&P 500 call and put options.

   (a) State the date that you selected. On a table, list the type of option (call or put), option price, and the calculated IV. In your calculation of the IV using the Hull software, you need to input the dividend yield on the index and the short-term rate of interest. Explain how you picked the dividend yield on the index and the short-term rate of interest. Employ a criterion of liquidity based on reported volume and open interest and confine your attention to liquid options.

   (b) Draw the IV of liquid options as a function of the in-the-moneyness, K/S. Explain the shape of the graph.

   (c) While recognizing that the graph in (b) need not be flat, pick the *relatively* most overpriced call/put. If you were to write this call/put, explain how you would delta-hedge it by specifying how many of the most underpriced/overpriced calls/puts you would buy or write.

(d) Look at the closing prices on the following day and state your profit and loss while ignoring transaction costs. How would transaction costs change your conclusion?

6. What option pricing biases are likely to be observed when:

(a) Both tails of the stock price distribution are thinner than those of the log-normal distribution?

(b) The right tail is thinner, and the left tail is fatter, than the right and left tails of a log-normal distribution?

(c) The stock price is positively correlated with volatility?

Chapter 13

Corporate Securities
and Credit Risk

Agenda

- Introduction
- Equity and discount bonds as options on firm assets
- Application: Pricing a corporate bond
- Subordinated debt
- Warrants
- Application: Pricing a warrant
- Callable bonds
- Callable convertible bonds
- Bank contingent capital — Co-co bonds
- Example: Optimal call, conversion and pricing of a callable convertible bond on a binomial tree

Introduction

Options are embedded in many corporate securities such as equity, bonds, warrants, callable bonds, and convertible bonds. In this lecture note, we apply what we have learned on option theory to the valuation of corporate securities. In the process, we highlight the credit risk of corporate securities.

The discussion of corporate securities in McDonald's Chapter 16 is excellent and more extensive than the corresponding discussion in Hull.

Equity and Discount Bonds as Options on Firm Assets

- Equity and bonds are viewed as options on the *value of the firm* (the value of the firm's expected future earnings). This approach highlights and quantifies the *credit risk* of corporate securities.
- In general, the yield of a 10-year corporate bond exceeds the Treasury Bill rate by a premium that consists of two components:

  (1) The *term premium*, defined as the difference between the yield of the 10-year Treasury bond and the Treasury Bill rate. Note that Treasury securities are default-free, unlike corporate bonds and government agency bonds that have credit risk.

  (2) The *credit risk premium*, defined as the difference between the yield of the 10-year corporate bond and the yield of a 10-year Treasury bond.

- We focus on the credit risk premium and sometimes suppress the term premium by assuming that the yield of all default-free bonds, such as Treasury bonds, is the same across maturities and is constant.
- First, we consider a firm that has only two types of claims: Common stock and one issue of discount bonds. Later on, we allow for junior (subordinated) debt.
- Assumptions and notation:

  — The firm has debt and equity, but no other claims.
  — The face value of outstanding debt is K.
  — The debt is zero-coupon and matures on date T.
  — The market value of the debt at time t is $B(t)$.
  — The market value of equity at time t is $E(t)$.
  — The value of the firm, $V(t)$, is the discounted value of all after-tax future earnings, before interest. $V(t) = E(t) + B(t)$.

- Draw the market value of debt and equity at the maturity date of the debt, as a function of the value of the firm:

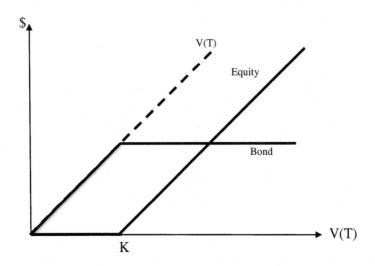

- Equity or common stock is a residual claim on the market value of the firm's net assets, provided the market value of the firm's assets exceed K, the *total* outstanding debt of the firm:

$$E(T) = \max[0, V(T) - K].$$

- Thus, *equity is a European call option on the firm value with strike the face value of outstanding debt and maturity equal to the debt maturity*:

$$E(t) = c(S = V(t), K, T).$$

- An increase in the volatility of future earnings, keeping the value of the firm constant, increases the value of equity and decreases the value of the debt.
- The value of the debt is the firm value minus the value of equity:

$$B(t) = V(t) - E(t).$$

- Applying the European put-call parity, we get:

$$B(t) = V(t) - E(t)$$

$$= V(t) - \left[V(t) - e^{-(T-t)r} K + p(S = V(t), K, T) \right]$$

$$= e^{-(T-t)r} K - p(S = V(t), K, T),$$

where p is the price of a European put on the firm value with strike the face value of outstanding debt and maturity equal to the debt maturity.

- If the debt were default-free, its value would be $e^{-(T-t)r} K$.
- The value of debt that is subject to default risk equals the value of default-free debt less the price of a European put on the firm value with strike the face value of outstanding debt and maturity equal to the debt maturity.
- The equity holders' limited liability amounts to a put option that allows the equity holders to "put" the value of the firm to the bond holders in lieu of paying the face value of the bond, if the value of the firm is lower than the face value of the bond.
- Effectively, the bond holders have written a European put to the equity holders and this reduces accordingly the market value of the debt.
- The bond yield, y, is defined by $B(t) = K \times e^{-(T-t)y}$. We take logs of both sides and solve for the yield as $y = (T-t)^{-1} \ln(K/B(t))$.
- In general, the amount by which the bond yield exceeds the yield of a same-maturity Treasury bond is called the *credit risk premium*.
- What is a CDS?
- What is the approximate value of a CDS on the bond over the life of the bond in this example?
- Why is the value only approximate?

Application: Pricing a Corporate Bond

- A firm has 1 million shares of stock with price $12 per share and a privately-placed discount bond with face value $3 million and maturity 5 years. The volatility of the rate of return on equity is 40%. (The volume can be measured either from past returns or as the IV from options on the equity.) The 5-year Treasury yield is 8%, annual c.c.
- Our task is to infer the market value of the bond, B.
- The market value of the firm is $V = 1$ million $\times 12 + B$.
- The underlying security is the value of the firm. The rate of return on the value of the firm is

$$
\frac{\text{change}(V)}{V} = \frac{\text{change}(B) + \text{change}(E)}{V}
$$

$$
= \frac{B}{V} \times \frac{\text{change}(B)}{B} + \frac{E}{V} \times \frac{\text{change}(E)}{E}
$$

$$
= \frac{B}{V} \times \text{ rate of bond return}
$$

$$
+ \frac{E}{V} \times \text{ rate of equity return.}
$$

- Let σ_V be the volatility of the rate of return on the value of the firm. This is *not the same* as the volatility of the rate of return on the equity, $\sigma_S = 0.40$.
- Assume that the value of the firm is log-normally distributed. (If this assumption is not realistic, we can resort to a binomial tree, as we do later on pages 212–219.)
- Viewing the equity as a call option on the value of the firm, we have

12 million

$$
= c_{\text{BSM}}(12 \text{ million} + B, K = 3 \text{ million}, T = 5 \text{ years}, \sigma_V), \qquad (1)
$$

where

$$d_1 = \frac{\ln\{(12 \text{ million} + B)/e^{-0.08 \times 5} \ 3 \text{ million}\}}{\sigma_V \sqrt{5}} + \frac{1}{2}\sigma_V \sqrt{5},$$

$$d_2 = d_1 - \sigma_V \sqrt{T}.$$

- If the volatility of the rate of return on the value of the firm, σ_V, were known, then we could solve for B by trial and error.
- In practice, σ_V, is not known but is related to the equity volatility, σ_S, as

$$0.40 = \sigma_S = \frac{nS + B}{nS} \ N(d_1) \ \sigma_V = \frac{12 \text{ million} + B}{12 \text{ million}} \ N(d_1) \ \sigma_V. \tag{2}$$

(You do not need to know how to derive Eq. (2) but do write it down on your crib sheet.)
- We have two equations, (1) and (2), and two unknowns, B and σ_V. We solve for B and σ_V by trial-and-error. (It is tedious but there are standard software out there that can do it for us.)
- The intuition behind Eq. (2) is as follows. Start with

$$\frac{\text{change}(V)}{V} = \frac{nS}{nS + B} \times \text{equity return} + \frac{B}{nS + B} \times \text{bond return}.$$

- If the default probability is zero, then volume(bond return) = 0

$$\sigma_V = \frac{nS}{nS + B} \times \sigma_S$$

and

$$\sigma_S = \frac{nS + B}{nS} \times \sigma_V.$$

- When we recognize the possibility of default, the bond holders share the risk with the stock holders and the stock price volume is adjusted downwards by the term $N(d_1)$.

Subordinated Debt

- Consider a firm with three classes of securities: senior debt, junior or subordinated debt, and equity (E).
- The senior debt has price B_S, face value K_S and zero coupons (coupons can be easily added to the example).
- Assume that the principal on the senior debt must be fully repaid before *anything* is paid to the subordinated debt holders (this strict priority rule can be relaxed in other examples).
- The junior debt has price B_J, face value K_J and zero coupons (coupons can be easily added to the example).
- If $V(T) < K_S$, the senior debt holders receive a pro rata claim on $V(T)$, the junior debt holders get nothing, and equity holders get nothing (bankruptcy costs can be added to the example).
- If $K_S < V(T) < K_S + K_J$, the senior debt holders receive K_S, the junior debt holders receive $V(T) - K_S$, and the equity holders get nothing.
- Draw the market value of equity and the junior and senior debt at the maturity date of the debt, as a function of the value of the firm:

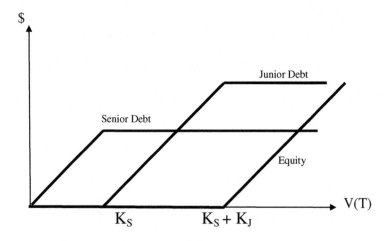

- Equity is still a call option, but it now has a higher strike price, $K_S + K_J$:

$$E = c(V, K_S + K_J).$$

- We price the junior debt by applying the following trick. We consider a portfolio that holds all the equity and junior bonds of this firm. At maturity, the value of this portfolio is:

$$\max[0, V(T) - K_S].$$

- The value of this portfolio T periods before maturity is:

$$E + B_J = c(V, K_S).$$

- Therefore, the value of the junior bond is:

$$
\begin{aligned}
B_J &= c(V, K_S) - E \\
&= c(V, K_S) - c(V, K_S + K_J).
\end{aligned}
$$

- The junior debt is a (bull) *call spread* on the value of the firm.
- When V is near K_S, does the value of the junior debt increase or decrease when volatility increases? Why? What is the vega?
- When V is near $K_S + K_J$, does the value the junior debt increase or decrease when volatility increases? Why? What is the vega?
- Finally, the value of the senior debt is:

$$B_S = V - (E + B_J) = V - c(V, K_S).$$

- As in the earlier application, we can price the senior and junior bonds by the BSM formula, if we know the market value of the equity and the volatility of its rate of return.
- In general, the junior and senior bonds have different maturities and we cannot apply the BSM formula. But we can price the senior and junior bonds on the binomial tree (see the example on page 205).

Warrants

- A warrant is a call option issued by the firm.
- A prime example of a warrant is an ESO, or *executive stock option*.
- If a warrant is exercised, the firm creates a new share of stock to give to the warrant holder (actually, the firm gives already shelf-registered shares).
- Unlike a regular call, when a warrant is exercised, the firm experiences *dilution* in ownership.
- Also, unlike a regular call, when a warrant is exercised, the exercise price is paid to the firm and increases the firm's value.
- Given:

  - ➤ Number of outstanding shares is 3 million.
  - ➤ Number of outstanding warrants is 2 million.
  - ➤ Strike price of each warrant is $20.
  - ➤ Therefore, the strike price of the warrant issue is 20×2 million $= \$40$ million.
  - ➤ The fraction of old and new shares owned by the warrant holders, if they exercise the warrants is $\alpha = (2)/(2+3) = 2/5$.

- We obtain the break-even value of the firm at maturity, at which the warrants are at the money by solving the equation $(2/5)(\widehat{V} + 40) = 40$. We find $\widehat{V} = 60$.
- Draw the value of equity and the warrant issue at maturity as a function of the firm value at maturity:

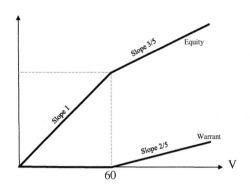

- Before we consider the general case, let us suppose that the value of the firm is, say, $V_T = \$100$ million on the warrants' expiration date. At expiration, the value of the warrant issue is:

$$W_T = \max\{0, (2/5)(100 + 40) - 40\} = \$16 \text{ million}.$$

- Each warrant is worth \$16 million/2 million $= \$8$ and should be exercised.
- The stock price at expiration, *right before exercise*, is $(100 - 16)/3 = \$28$. The stock price at expiration, *right after exercise*, is $(100 + 40)/5 = \$28$, the same!
- How does an unsophisticated warrant holder who observes the stock price \$28 know whether to exercise a warrant at expiration?
- Simply by choosing the larger of zero and $\$28 - \$20 = \$8$. The warrant holder should exercise the warrant and the warrant price is \$8.

General case

- If the warrant issue is exercised, the new shares are worth $(2/5)\{V(T) + 40 \text{ million}\}$.
- The total value of the warrants at expiration (T) is:

$$
\begin{aligned}
W(T) &= \max[0, (2/5)\{V(T) + 40 \text{ million}\} - 40 \text{ million}] \\
&= \max[0, (2/5)V(T) - (3/5)40 \text{ million}] \\
&= (2/5)\max[0, V(T) - 60 \text{ million}].
\end{aligned}
$$

- The warrant holders' claim is a call option on fraction $2/5$ of the firm with strike price 60 million.
- If the value of the firm is log-normally distributed, the total value of the warrants prior to maturity is given by the BSM equation.

Application: Pricing a Warrant

- A firm has 3 million shares of stock with price $35 per share. The firm also has a privately-placed European warrant issue with strike $40 million maturity in 3 years from now, and exercisable into 2 million shares of stock. The volatility of the rate of return on equity is 40%. The 3-year Treasury yield is 8%, annual c.c.
- Our task is to infer the warrant price.
- From the relation $V = nS + W$, we have

$$V = 3 \times 35 + (2/5)c_{\text{BSM}}(V, 60, \tau = 3 \text{ years}, \sigma_V). \qquad (3)$$

- Consider first the case where we pretend that we know σ_V just to illustrate the approach. Then Eq. (3) has only one unknown, V.
- We can find V by trial-and-error: guess a value of V that equates the left and right-hand sides of Eq. (3).
- The equation can be solved by using software such as the *Excel-Solver* routine.
- Once we find V, we obtain the value of the warrants as $W = V - 3 \times 35$.
- Consider next the realistic case that σ_V is not known. The volatilities σ_S and σ_V are related as follows:

$$\sigma_v = \frac{\sigma_S \times n \times S}{V[1 - \alpha N(d_1)]}, \qquad (4)$$

where

$$d_1 = \frac{\ln\left(\frac{\alpha V}{(1-\alpha)Ke^{-r\tau}}\right)}{\sigma_V \sqrt{\tau}} + \frac{\sigma_V \sqrt{\tau}}{2}.$$

(You need not know how to derive Eq. (4) but write it down on your crib sheet for the final.)
- We have two unknowns, V and σ_V and two equations (3) and (4). We solve for V and σ_V numerically.

- Once we solve for V, we obtain the value of the warrants as $W = V - nS$.
- In practice, ESOs and most warrants are American. We either use the BSM equation as a first approximation or solve the problem on a binomial tree.
- *Caution*: It turns out that the ESOs are not always exercised optimally. Sometimes they are exercised too early and other times too late. In practice, when we price ESOs we take the observed exercise practices into account.
- Since warrants are American, it is more realistic to price them on a binomial tree. See problem #1 on the 2010 final exam.
- What is a put warrant? See problem #13 on the 2011 final exam.

Callable Bonds

- Most corporate bonds and government agency bonds are callable.
- The bondholders "write" an (embedded) call option to the issuer of the bond. The issuer can buy back the bond at a pre-specified price — the *call price*.
- The market price of the bond reflects this option.
- This call option usually can be exercised only after a "call protection" period of time.
- A typical schedule of call prices of a 20-year callable bond with face value 100 reads in *Moody's Manual* as follows:

  — Years 1–5: under call protection
  — Years 6–10: callable at 105
  — Years 11–15: callable at 103
  — Years 16–20: callable at par (100).

- At call, the bondholders receive the call price plus the coupon accrued since the last coupon payment.
- If management represents the interests of the equity holders, as it should, management should call the bond if the market value of the bond tends to exceed the call price plus accrued interest.
- In practice, refinancing costs, tax considerations, appeasement of bond holders, and plain incompetence play a role.
- What are the market conditions under which the market value of the bond tends to exceed the call price and prompts the management to call the bond?
- We defer pricing a callable bond until we introduce convertible bonds. Then, we illustrate, by example, the optimal call, optimal conversion, and pricing of corporate bonds.

Callable Convertible Bonds

- A convertible corporate bond gives its holder an option to convert the bond into a pre-specified number of shares.
- The conversion feature is American.
- All convertible bonds are also callable. (However, many callable bonds are not convertible.)
- If management decides to call the bond, it has to give typically 4–6 weeks "call notice" to the bond holders. If the bond holders do not convert, then the management calls the bond at the end of the notice period.
- Why do firms issue convertible bonds? Do convertible bonds make economic sense?
- Since both the call and conversion features are American, the BSM pricing equation is inadequate to price them. We illustrate their optimal call, conversion and pricing on a binomial tree.

Bank Contingent Capital

- One form of Tier II bank capital that has seen tremendous growth since the 2007–2009 financial crisis is the contingent convertible bond, or Co-co.
- In bad times, a trigger which can be based either on capital ratios or the bank share price automatically triggers conversion of the Co-co into bank equity, thereby avoiding the costs of financial distress and freeing up debt capacity.
- In good times, a Co-co is a bond and provides tax deductibility of interest expense and the discipline imposed on management by draining free cashflow.
- *Related securities*: Put able bonds. They give the right to *management* to convert the bond into a pre-specified number of shares. Also put warrants.
- *Catastrophe bonds*: Automatically become equity if a certain natural disaster hits the (typically, insurance) company.

Example: Optimal call, conversion and pricing of a callable convertible bond on a binomial tree

- A firm has two corporate claims, equity and one issue of callable convertible bonds.
- Equity consists of 150 shares of common stock, paying no dividends.
- The bond issue consists of 100 bonds, 10% coupon payable once a year, face value $1000 each, callable at $1100 each, and maturing in two years. A bond is convertible into one share of stock.
- We assume that the current value of the firm is $200,000, net of the current coupon payment. On a 2-year binomial tree with two annual steps, the parameters are given as $u = 1.5$, $d = 0.5$, $\bar{r} = 1.08$, and therefore the risk-adjusted probability is $p = \frac{\bar{r}-d}{u-d} = 0.58$.
- In this example, we assume that we know the value of the firm and the volatility of the rate of return on the value of the firm. We build a binomial tree and price the equity and bond.

- This approach can be applied to use information from the stock price and its return volatility to price a bond, as on page 218 of this chapter.
- Let us build the binomial tree for the value of the firm and the value of the convertible bond.
- The *conversion ratio* $\frac{100}{150+100} = 0.4$ is the fraction of the old plus new equity that the bondholders have, if they convert.
- Thus, at the node uu, if the bondholders convert, they get $0.4 \times 425 = 170$ thousand plus the coupon.

$$u = 1.5 \ d = 0.5 \ \bar{r} = 1.08 \ p = 0.58$$

- Numbers in thousands
- Conversion ratio: $\frac{100}{150+100} = 40\%$.

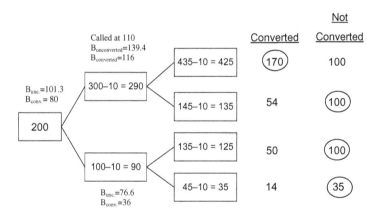

- Will the bondholders voluntarily convert at u?
- After the coupon is received at time 1, the *unconverted* value of the bond at u is:

$$B_u = \frac{0.58 \times 170{,}000 + 0.42 \times 100{,}000}{1.08} + \frac{10{,}000}{1.08} = \$139{,}440.$$

- The conversion value at u is:

$$0.4 \times \$290{,}000 = \$116{,}000.$$

- *So the bondholders will not convert voluntarily.* (We know this even without this calculation because the stock does not pay dividends.)
- The firm optimally chooses to call the bond at u. Let us see why.
- If the firm calls, the bondholders can either deliver the bond for the call price of $110, or convert and receive shares worth $116.
- The bondholders optimally convert, thus giving up securities worth $139,440 for shares worth $116,000.
- This results in a transfer of $23,440 from the bondholders to the shareholders.
- *Therefore, at this node, it is optimal for the firm to call and force conversion.*
- This type of conversion is called "forced conversion" because the bond holders are forced to convert to avoid having the bond called.
- At the node d, the unconverted value of the bond is:

$$B_d = \frac{0.58 \times 100,000 + 0.42 \times 35,000}{1.08} + \frac{10,000}{1.08} = \$76,574.$$

- The converted value of the bond is $0.4 \times \$90,000 = \$36,000$.
- Since the unconverted value of the bond is greater than the converted value, the bondholders do not wish to convert.
- Since the call value (or, in this case the firm value of 90,000) is greater than the bond value (unconverted), the firm *chooses not to* call.
- We can now price the unconverted bond with two periods to go:

$$B = \frac{0.58 \times 116,000 + 0.42 \times 76,574}{1.08} + \frac{10,000}{1.08} = \$101,334.$$

- If the bondholders convert, they get $0.4 \times \$200,000 = \$80,000$. Therefore, the bondholders choose not to convert.
- Also, since $101,334 is less than the call price, the firm does not wish to call.
- The total value of the callable convertible bonds with two periods to go is $101,334.

- The value of the stock today is $200,000 - $101,334 = $98,666. The share price is $98,666/150 = $658.
- If the observed value of the stock today is different than $98,666, we pick a different initial value of the firm and redo the calculations.
- The example illustrates a *forced conversion*, which is what usually happens.
- Right before *ex dividend* dates, we may have a *voluntary conversion*: The bondholders choose to convert even though they have not received call notice, in order to capture the dividend.
- Nowadays, most convertibles are *dividend-protected*: When a bond is converted, the bondholders receive not only the stock but also all past dividends.
- If a hedge fund buys the entire issue of the convertible bond, how many shares of stock does the fund have to short in order to hedge its position?
- In the state u, the share price is

$$(\$290,000 - \$116,000)/150 = \$1160.$$

- In the state d, the share price is

$$(\$90,000 - \$76,500)/150 = \$90.$$

- The hedge fund needs to short N_S shares such that

$$116,000 + 10,000 - N_S \times 1,160 = 76,500 + 10,000 - N_S \times 90$$

or,

$$N_S = \frac{116,000 - 76,500}{1,160 - 90} = 36.9.$$

- The hedge fund needs to short approximately 37 shares.

- An alternative way to determine the number of shares (N_S) the fund needs to sell is as follows:

— The hedge ratio of the convertible bond is

$$\Delta_{\text{CONV}} = \frac{116,000 + 10,000 - 76,500 - 10,000}{290,000 - 90,000}.$$

— The hedge ratio of one share of stock is

$$\Delta_{\text{SHARE}} = \frac{1,160 - 90}{290,000 - 90,000}.$$

— The portfolio is delta-neutral, provided

$$1 \times \Delta_{\text{CONV}} - N_S \times \Delta_{\text{SHARE}} = 0$$

or

$$1 \times \frac{116,000 + 10,000 - 76,500 - 10,000}{290,000 - 90,000} - N_S$$

$$\times \frac{1,160 - 90}{290,000 - 90,000} = 0$$

with solution $N_S = 36.9$, as before.

Assignment 8

1. (*Pricing equity as a call option on the assets*) ABC Corporation has assets of market value $100 million. The return on the assets has volatility 20% per year. ABC's capital structure consists of debt and one million shares of common stock. The debt is 100,000 zero-coupon bonds, maturing in 2 years, each with face value $1000. Assume that the risk-free interest rate is a constant 4% (annualized, c.c.). Because of its bond covenants, ABC will not pay dividends over the next two years.

   (a) Apply the BSM equation to price one share of ABC common stock.

   (b) Apply the BSM equation to price one ABC zero-coupon bond. Calculate also the bond yield and the default risk premium.

2. (*Pricing a corporate bond from equity data*) In real life, we do not directly observe the market value of a firm's assets. Instead, we observe the book value of the assets as an imperfect proxy for the market value of the firm's assets. However, we observe the market value of the equity and also estimate the volatility of the equity return. By treating the equity as a call option on the firm's assets, we can use the BSM equation to estimate the firm's assets and the value of the corporate bond. In this problem, we make the task a little easier by assuming that we know the volatility of the rate of return of the firm's assets.

   XYZ Corporation's capital structure consists of debt and 500,000 shares of common stock. The debt consists of 50,000 zero-coupon bonds, maturing in 2 years, each with a face value of $1000. XYZ's common stock trades at $40 per share. Assume that the volatility of the rate of return of the assets of XYZ is 25% per year. The risk-free rate is a constant 4% (annualized, c.c.). Because of its bond covenant, XYZ will not pay dividends over the next two years. Our goal is to price the corporate bond. Let us approach the problem in three steps.

(a) Treating the equity as a call option on the firm's value, what is the underlying asset of the call option? What is the volatility of the underlying asset? What is the strike price of the "call"?

(b) Based on the market value of the equity, use the BSM equation to find the implied value of XYZ's assets.

(c) What should the market value of one corporate bond be?

3. (*Warrant pricing*) The capital structure of ABC consists of 400,000 shares of common stock and 200,000 warrants 8 months from maturity, with strike price $100 per warrant. The ABC stock trades at $98 per share. Assume that the volatility of the return of ABC's total assets is $\sigma_V = 15\%$ (annualized). The risk-free rate, (annualized, continuous compounding) is 5%.

(a) What is the value of each single warrant?

(b) Supposing that we have 1000 warrants instead of 200,000 warrants, while all other variables above (except for V) stay the same, re-calculate the value of each single warrant.

(c) Still assuming 1000 warrants, do you expect ABC's stock return volatility to be close to 15%? Do not use any formula — briefly present your intuition.

(d) Assume that ABC's *stock return* volatility is 15%. Use the BSM equation to calculate the value of a call option on ABC's stock with the same strike price and maturity as the warrant. Is the result close to your answer to part (b) above? Intuitively, why should you expect this?

4. (*Pricing warrants on a binomial tree*) A firm has value $100 million. Each year, the value of the firm increases or decreases by 20%, before dividends. The total amount of dividend paid by the firm each year is $5 million, and is paid once a year. The annual simple interest rate is 10%.

(a) Suppose that the firm is all equity-financed and has one million shares. Price a two-year European call with strike $100 on a two-step binomial tree. (Assume that, if you exercise the call at the end of a year, you receive *cum dividend* stock.)

(b) Now, suppose that the firm has 1 million shares, and a European warrant issue with strike price $50 million exercisable into 1 million shares. Price the warrant issue on the binomial tree. Also find the price per share on the binomial tree. Finally explain how you hedge the warrant by using the equity of the firm.

(c) Re-price the warrant in the last step, assuming that it is American.

5. (*Pricing callable convertibles on a binomial tree.*) A firm's value will either increase by 50% or decrease by 40% over each of the next two years. The market value of the assets is $4 million. The simple annual risk-free rate is 10%. The firm has 2000 callable convertible bonds that pay an annual 10% coupon. These bonds have a face value of $1000, and have a call price of $1100. Moreover, each of these bonds is convertible at any time into a single share of the firm's common stock. There are currently 3000 shares of common stock outstanding. For simplicity, you should assume that the conversion of the bonds can be made only as a block.

(a) Find the value of a single callable convertible bond.

(b) Find the value of a single share of stock.

Printed in the United States
By Bookmasters